Think Like A Modern Guru

Alex Telman

Published by Alex Telman, 2024.

While every precaution has been taken in the preparation of this book, the publisher assumes no responsibility for errors or omissions, or for damages resulting from the use of the information contained herein.

THINK LIKE A MODERN GURU

First edition. December 16, 2024.

Copyright © 2024 Alex Telman.

ISBN: 979-8230543503

Written by Alex Telman.

Table of Contents

Introduction: Embracing the Modern Guru Mindset

Wake Up and Step into the Guru's Mindset

This isn't some self-help fluff about dreaming of being "better." If you're expecting herbal tea, hours of meditation, or chanting in a quiet room, stop reading now. But if you're ready to wake up, take responsibility for who you are, and change how you show up in the world, you're in the right place.

You're about to learn how to think like a modern guru. And let me be clear: this isn't an easy road. No one's handing you a certificate of enlightenment, and there won't be a parade when you "get it." The real work doesn't happen while sitting in lotus position. It happens when you stop making excuses, get off your ass, and take action. It's about owning your growth and quitting the blame game.

Want to master yourself? Be the best version of you every day? Then be prepared to fight for it. True mastery takes grit, resilience, and a mindset that's willing to challenge itself, confront its own bullshit, and grow in ways you never thought possible.

This book isn't for the weak. If you want comfort and easy answers, it's the wrong place. But if you're ready to face life's toughest challenges and still come out on top, if you want to become your own guru, then keep reading.

Why a Modern Guru Mindset?

There's a reason the term "guru" carries weight. It's not just about someone sitting at the top of a mountain, draped in a robe, dispensing wisdom to followers. **The true guru** isn't someone who's "better" than you or me. They're someone who's done the work. They've faced their demons, mastered their own mind, and created a life of purpose and service.

But let's get one thing straight: **being a guru isn't about achieving perfection**—it's about mastering the basics of life in ways that allow you to continually grow and evolve. It's about taking full responsibility for your thoughts, emotions, and actions. It's about understanding that you don't need to seek out some external savior to guide you—you already have the answers within yourself.

Think about this: every major leader in history, from Buddha to Gandhi to Martin Luther King Jr., **was a modern guru in their own right.** They didn't sit around waiting for life to give them permission to make a difference—they took action. They didn't wait for their circumstances to align perfectly, they didn't wait for someone else's approval. They decided that the world needed something, and they were going to be the ones to provide it.

The modern guru mindset is **about realizing your own power**—it's about stepping up to the plate and swinging for the fences. It's about taking full responsibility for the life you create, and **refusing to let fear, doubt, or uncertainty hold you back**. The guru doesn't look for excuses—they look for solutions.

That's the mindset we're going to develop in this book.

What You'll Learn

In these pages, you'll discover that thinking like a modern guru is far less about some far-off mystical realm and much more about practical, everyday principles that can transform your life **right now.** No more waiting. No more wishing. It's time to start living the life you're capable of. It's time to start thinking like the guru you were always meant to be.

We'll break down the key qualities that make a guru a guru:

- **Self-Mastery:** You'll learn how to take control of your thoughts, emotions, and actions, so they work for you, not against you.
- **Resilience and Strength:** The guru doesn't shy away from life's challenges. They face adversity with mental toughness, emotional resilience, and a deep commitment to self-growth.
- **Living With Purpose:** We'll explore how the guru lives with a

clear sense of mission, with deep focus, and with service to others at the core of everything they do.

- **Legacy:** You'll understand how a modern guru doesn't just live for themselves—they create a legacy that impacts others and continues long after they're gone.

More importantly, you'll understand **how to integrate these principles into your own life.** Because you don't need to be some ancient mystic to start living with power, clarity, and purpose. The guru mindset is **accessible to you, right now.**

The Guru's Journey: An Ongoing Path

One of the biggest misconceptions about gurus is that they have somehow "arrived." That they've reached some enlightened state and are now **done.** But that's where the real misunderstanding lies. **The true guru knows that the journey never ends.** There is no final destination. The path to mastery is continuous. It's a process of growth, learning, and evolving, with each day presenting a new opportunity to expand.

If you think you'll ever reach some kind of ultimate "level" where you stop learning, where you stop growing, then you're not ready to be a guru. **Mastery is a constant journey.** And the more you embrace this idea, the more you'll realize that **each challenge, each setback, each failure, is just another lesson** to deepen your understanding of yourself and the world around you.

In this book, we'll dive into the practical tools you need to develop the mental toughness, emotional resilience, and focus that **will propel you forward.** We'll give you the frameworks to move through life's inevitable challenges, with a mindset that turns every obstacle into an opportunity for growth. It's not about avoiding suffering or difficulty—it's about learning how to **embrace it** as part of the process.

Stop Looking Outside, Start Looking Within

Another major principle of the guru mindset is realizing that **you already have the power** within you. You don't need to keep looking outside for guidance, validation, or permission. Sure, you can learn from others, but at the end of the day, **you're the one who decides who you become.**

We've all been conditioned to seek out gurus—whether they're in the form of self-help books, motivational speakers, or influencers with millions of followers. But here's the truth: **The real guru lives inside you.** You've been looking for answers in the wrong places. **It's time to become your own guide.**

This is about shifting your mindset. Instead of asking, "What can I get from others?" ask yourself, "What can I give?" The true guru gives freely, without expecting anything in return. They serve because it is their highest calling, and they create with the intention to uplift others.

And it's not just about grand gestures or philosophical musings. **It's about making real, concrete shifts in how you live, act, and show up in the world.**

What You Can Expect

Let's get this straight: if you think this book is going to be a collection of feel-good fluff or easy solutions, you're mistaken. If you're looking for a miracle pill to fix your life, you're in the wrong place. This isn't about superficial affirmations or waiting for the universe to give you a sign. You came here because you want something real. Something concrete. Something that works. And that's exactly what I'm giving you.

You're here because you want to become a *Modern Guru*—someone who's got their shit together, who isn't controlled by their circumstances, who has the mental and emotional clarity to navigate through the chaos of life. If you're serious, if you're hungry for real transformation, you've come to the right place.

But understand this: the path to this transformation won't be easy. There will be no hand-holding. There will be no fluff. You will be called to examine the deepest parts of yourself, to challenge your old habits, your old beliefs, and your old behaviors. And you will make decisions, real decisions, to start living from a place of power and clarity.

So what can you expect from this book?

1. **A Blueprint for Mental Mastery** We're going to break down how your mind works. We'll tear through the layers of doubt, fear, and confusion that have been holding you back. You're going to understand how your thoughts shape your reality, and how to take control of them. But I'm not talking about "positive thinking" or "manifesting your dreams." I'm talking about *mental mastery*—the ability to direct your mind with precision, cut through the noise, and make decisions that align with your highest self.
    - **The key theme here is control.** Not control over others. But control over your mind. Over your reactions. Over your decisions.
2. **Tools for Silence in a World Full of Noise** This world is loud. It's designed to be distracting. Whether it's social media, your boss, your family, or the constant notifications pinging on your phone,

there's no shortage of distractions. And if you can't manage the noise, you'll never find the clarity you need to live with purpose.

The Modern Guru knows how to quiet their mind in a chaotic world. And in this book, you'll learn how to do that too. Through proven practices like meditation, mindfulness, and focused breathing, you'll start cultivating stillness. You'll start learning how to shut out the distractions and **center yourself**—something that's no longer optional, it's mandatory for anyone who wants to thrive in today's world.

- **The key theme here is focus.** If you can't focus, you're done. The world will dictate your life for you. If you're going to master your life, you need to master your ability to focus.

1. **Emotional Resilience: How to Bounce Back and Keep Moving** Life is not a straight line. It's full of setbacks, disappointments, failures. The world will knock you down, over and over again. But the Modern Guru doesn't stay down. They get up. Every. Single. Time.

You will learn how to build the emotional resilience needed to push through pain, disappointment, and fear. This is about developing a mindset that refuses to stay stuck in negativity. It's about learning how to turn pain into power. And no, this isn't some "positive vibes only" nonsense. It's real. Raw. And unapologetically honest.

- **The key theme here is resilience.** You will get knocked down, but you will get up faster. You will learn how to take the punches and use them to fuel your growth.

1. **Mastering the Power of Action** A guru doesn't sit around waiting for things to happen. They don't wait for the universe to deliver. They **take action**. Big action. Bold action. Action that's rooted in deep clarity and personal power. You will learn how to take decisive

steps toward your goals, no matter how impossible they may seem.

This is where many people fail. They get paralyzed by indecision, they wait for the perfect moment, they seek permission, they second-guess themselves. A Modern Guru doesn't operate that way. Once they've made a decision, they go. And they go fast.

- **The key theme here is action.** You're going to stop procrastinating. You're going to start executing. And you're going to do it with absolute commitment.

1. **Spiritual Wisdom for the Modern World** This isn't just about success, happiness, or achievement. It's about something deeper. It's about aligning your actions with a deeper sense of meaning and purpose. A Modern Guru has a connection to something greater than themselves. They understand that life is more than just what's happening on the surface. They operate from a higher place—one that's rooted in spiritual wisdom.

You're going to learn how to tap into this deeper wisdom. You'll begin to understand the power of **being in alignment**—aligning your actions, thoughts, and emotions with your deepest values. You'll get clear on your purpose and how to live it every day. This isn't some abstract idea—it's a practical, grounded way of living that will change the way you approach your life.

- **The key theme here is alignment.** The Modern Guru is not scattered. They don't live with conflicting values. They know who they are and what they stand for. They're aligned with their highest self and their deepest purpose.

1. **Creating Your Legacy** You're not here to just live. You're here to leave a mark. A Modern Guru doesn't just live for the moment—they live for the future. They live with an eye on their legacy. And you need to do the same. This book will show you how to think beyond your immediate needs and start focusing on the long-term impact you want to have on the world.

This isn't about material success or fleeting fame. This is about creating a legacy of impact—whether it's through your family, your career, your community, or something else. You will learn how to craft a life that leaves a lasting impression, a life that's full of meaning and contribution.

- **The key theme here is legacy.** What are you leaving behind? The Modern Guru doesn't just think about today; they think about tomorrow. They live in such a way that their impact is felt long after they're gone.

In this book, you're going to go from someone who's **reacting** to life to someone who's **leading** it. You're going to learn how to become a Modern Guru—how to master your mind, take control of your emotions, and make powerful, purposeful decisions. You'll walk away with the tools, the mindset, and the wisdom you need to live a life that's not just successful, but meaningful.

You're going to step into your power. You're going to make things happen. And most importantly, you're going to do it on your terms.

What's Coming Next

In the chapters ahead, we'll walk through the specific steps and practices that will help you develop the mindset of a modern guru. You'll learn how to master your thoughts and emotions. You'll learn how to face adversity with strength. You'll learn how to **live a life of purpose** and service to others.

But don't expect to "get it" all at once. This isn't some quick-fix program. **This is a lifetime commitment to growth.** The principles in this book won't make you an overnight success, but they'll set you on the path to continuous improvement, deeper fulfillment, and **true inner power**.

The journey begins with one simple question: **Are you ready?**

If you're ready to stop making excuses, stop waiting for permission, and step into your true potential—then let's begin. The path to thinking like a modern guru starts **right now**. And it's going to be a hell of a ride.

So, are you ready to stop wasting time? Ready to get serious about your own transformation?

Good. Let's begin. Let's get to work. No excuses. No bulldust. You're going to leave this book as someone who is **in control**. Ready? Let's go.

Chapter 1: The Mind of the Guru: Cultivating Inner Peace

Part 1: The Nature of a Calm Mind

————

Listen up. This isn't the time for fluff. If you want to master your life, you need to start with mastering your mind. Period. Everything else, your health, your relationships, your work, it all comes second to your mind. If your mind isn't in control, you'll always be reacting to the world instead of shaping it. That's the cold, hard truth.

We live in a world that is designed to distract you. Everywhere you turn, there's noise—whether it's social media, work pressure, family demands, or just the relentless barrage of "stuff" you're supposed to care about. It's a constant stream of input that never stops. No wonder people are anxious, stressed, and overwhelmed. It's exhausting.

But a *Modern Guru* isn't exhausted. They're calm. They're still. And that's where you need to start: **the power of a calm mind.**

The Importance of Mental Stillness in a Chaotic World

Here's the deal: if your mind isn't still, you can't see clearly. Period. You're constantly reacting to the noise around you. You can't think straight. You're constantly distracted, anxious, or chasing the next thing to quiet the storm inside your head. You're not in control. The world is.

Think about it: when was the last time you really, truly sat with yourself and didn't feel the need to check your phone or rush to the next task? You might feel like your mind is "busy" with a million things, but that's the problem. **Busy doesn't equal productive.** It doesn't equal calm. It doesn't equal power. All it means is that you're a slave to your own thoughts and the outside world.

Mental stillness is where clarity begins.

You can't create anything new or meaningful in your life if you're constantly reacting. You can't solve problems effectively if your mind is cluttered. And you sure as hell can't lead others if you're not in control of your own thoughts. *The guru mindset* is about mental discipline. It's about achieving that state of inner stillness no matter what's going on outside.

This doesn't mean shutting yourself off from the world or avoiding responsibility. It means mastering your ability to focus. To center yourself. To create space between stimulus and response. To make choices instead of being driven by impulse or emotion.

And if you're serious about becoming a Modern Guru, this is non-negotiable. **You must cultivate mental stillness in a chaotic world.**

Peace of Mind vs. Calmness of Mind

Now, let's break this down because it's critical. You might think you're after "peace of mind," but that's not it. The goal isn't peace of mind—it's calmness of mind.

Peace of mind is an external state. It's a temporary absence of conflict or stress. When things are going your way, you feel peaceful. When everything is perfect, you feel peaceful. But let's be clear: *peace of mind is fleeting.* It depends on the external world lining up with your expectations. It's an illusion. You're relying on things outside of you to determine whether or not you're peaceful. And that's dangerous. Because as soon as something goes wrong, your peace of mind is shattered.

Now, **calmness of mind**, that's a different beast. Calmness of mind comes from within. It's not dependent on what's going on around you. It's about being **able to stay clear, centered, and focused even when the world is falling apart.**

Think about a storm. You're standing in the middle of it—wind howling, rain pouring down. That's the world. It's chaotic. But deep inside the storm, at the very center, there's a place of calmness. The eye of the storm. And that's where you want to be.

A Modern Guru isn't phased by the chaos. They don't need the world to stop moving to find peace. They can stay calm no matter what's going on. This is the mental mastery you need to develop if you want to take control of your life.

The First Step: Creating Space

You're going to need to practice. I'm not going to lie to you and tell you this is going to happen overnight. It's going to take work. But the first step is **creating space.**

I know, I know. You don't have time. Your to-do list is a mile long. You're already stretched thin. But I'm going to be blunt: if you don't make time for this, you're screwed. Because without this, everything else you do will be reactive, scattered, and unfocused.

You need to create moments in your day to quiet the noise. It doesn't matter if you're meditating for five minutes in the morning or taking a 10-minute walk in silence. You need to start carving out **space** where your mind isn't being bombarded with distractions.

Action Step: Take five minutes tomorrow morning and sit in complete silence. No phone, no distractions. Just you and your breath. Focus on your breathing. If your mind starts to wander, bring it back to your breath. Don't judge the thoughts that come up. Just notice them and let them pass. Five minutes. That's all. And do it consistently for the next week. Watch what happens.

The Key to Clarity: Mindfulness

Mindfulness isn't some fluffy term from a yoga retreat. It's a real, practical skill that sharpens your mind and keeps you grounded. It's the ability to be fully present in the moment without judgment or distraction.

A guru doesn't get lost in their thoughts. They're not living in the past or the future. They're **here.** Right now. Present.

If you're not practicing mindfulness, you're not practicing mental mastery. The minute you stop paying attention, the minute your mind drifts off into the past or future, you lose clarity. You lose control. And you lose your power. That's why mindfulness is non-negotiable if you want to develop the calmness of mind that a Modern Guru possesses.

Action Step: When you're eating, just eat. When you're walking, just walk. When you're talking to someone, just listen. If your mind drifts to the past or future, *bring it back to the present.* Start with small moments throughout your day, and build the habit of staying present.

Mental Toughness: The Key to Sustaining Calmness

A calm mind doesn't just come from passive sitting or waiting for peace to come to you. It's the result of **mental toughness**. It's the ability to maintain your focus, your presence, and your emotional state regardless of the challenges or distractions around you.

When things go south—when you get bad news, when things don't go your way—that's when the rubber hits the road. Anyone can look calm when everything is going smoothly. But can you stay calm when things get tough? Can you still think clearly when you're in the middle of a storm?

That's what the Modern Guru can do. They've trained themselves to keep their calm in the face of adversity.

Here's the bottom line: if you want to master your life, you've got to start by mastering your mind. You can't afford to be a slave to your thoughts, emotions, and reactions. You need to cultivate stillness in a chaotic world. And that doesn't come from relying on external circumstances to be perfect. That comes from within.

A Modern Guru isn't just peaceful when things are going well. They're calm when the world is crashing down around them. They've learned to manage their mind, control their focus, and stay grounded, no matter what.

So, what are you waiting for? Get to work. Your mental clarity is the key to your freedom. **It's time to take control.**

Part 2: Overcoming Mental Noise

———

Let's cut to the chase. If you want to make any real progress in life—whether it's building wealth, getting healthier, having better relationships, or just being at peace with yourself—you've got to deal with **mental noise**. And not just deal with it, *quiet it*. Right now, that noise is your biggest enemy.

It's time to face the truth: your mind is on a constant loop of thoughts. You think you're in control. You think you can direct your mind like a well-trained dog, but the reality is much different. It's more like a barking, unruly pack of dogs, each pulling you in a different direction. They're yapping all day and night, telling you what you *should* do, what you *should've* done, what's *coming next*. And most of the time, you don't even know why these thoughts are running your show.

Now, imagine if you could get that pack of dogs to sit down, shut up, and stay quiet. What would that feel like? To be in control. To be the one calling the shots, instead of just reacting to the next crazy thought that hits you. **That's what a Modern Guru does.**

The goal here isn't just to shut off all thoughts—because let's be honest, that's impossible. But it is to **quiet the noise**. To stop living on autopilot, reacting to every little thing. You need to *calm the chaos* in your mind before you can make any meaningful change in your life. So let's dive in.

How to Identify and Quiet the Inner Chatter

Let's start with the basics. The first step is **awareness**. You can't quiet the noise if you're not even aware of it. The problem is, most people don't notice the constant stream of thoughts going through their head. They've been listening to it so long that they think it's just how things are. It's like living in a house with a loud, broken heater that never shuts off—you don't even realize how loud it is until you turn it off.

Your first task: *Pay attention*. I mean really pay attention to your thoughts. When you wake up in the morning, are your thoughts immediately racing to everything you need to do that day? Are you thinking about the things you regret from yesterday? Or are you already anticipating stress from tomorrow? That's the noise I'm talking about.

Here's the thing. **Most of the time, your thoughts are not serving you.** They're just running in circles. You're replaying conversations, rehashing past mistakes, worrying about the future—all while ignoring the present. And none of that noise is helping you move forward. It's just filling your head with junk.

So step one is simple: **Notice the noise.** When you catch yourself spiraling into these mental loops, stop and say, "Not today, buddy." You don't need to follow every thought like it's the next episode in a TV series.

The Role of Thought Patterns in Creating Stress

Alright, now let's talk about why that noise matters. It's not just *annoying*, it's dangerous. Your thoughts directly influence how you feel. When you're stuck in these looping thoughts, they create **stress**. You start to feel anxious, restless, frustrated—like you can't get ahead of yourself, like the world is moving too fast.

You've probably had moments when you've thought about a problem over and over, and then suddenly, it's like the problem gets *bigger*. The stress grows. It spirals. You start imagining all the worst-case scenarios, and before you know it, you're in full-blown panic mode.

This is the **power of thought patterns**. These repetitive, automatic thoughts can trap you in a state of anxiety or fear. It's like a hamster wheel that never stops turning. You don't even realize that it's your thoughts that are keeping you on that wheel, and you're just running in place, burning out and getting nowhere.

Let me break it down for you: **You create your stress**. Sure, external events trigger your stress, but it's the *thoughts* you attach to those events that really drive the anxiety. The situation itself doesn't control how you feel. Your interpretation of it does.

Example: Let's say you get an email from your boss saying, "We need to talk." What's the first thing that happens in your head? "Oh God, I'm getting fired! What did I do wrong? I'm going to lose my job! My whole life is going to fall apart!" And bam—your mind is in full panic mode.

But here's the truth: **You don't know what's going to happen.** You've just let your mind run wild. The situation hasn't even unfolded yet, but your thoughts have already created the stress.

The key here is understanding: your thoughts are the cause of your stress, not the world around you. And if you can get a grip on your thoughts, you can *defuse* that stress before it takes hold of you.

Action Steps to Quiet Your Mind

Okay, enough theory. Let's get to the meat of this: how do you shut that mental chatter up? I'm going to give you some tools that you can start using today. No excuses.

1. The "Stop" Technique

This is the first tool you need. Whenever you catch yourself in a loop of thoughts, repeat the word "Stop" in your head. You're not trying to silence yourself. You're interrupting the cycle. You're not letting your thoughts take you wherever they want to go. You're asserting control. When you notice your mind running wild, mentally yell "STOP" at it.

It's simple, but it works. The idea here is to break the automatic flow of thoughts, to regain control. Don't let your mind dictate your mood.

2. Breathwork: The Ultimate Interruptor

When you say "stop," the next move is to take a deep breath. Slow. Deep. Focused. In through your nose, out through your mouth. Repeat. You're grounding yourself in your body, not in your runaway thoughts. Breathing forces you to be present. It's almost impossible to focus on your breath and your racing thoughts at the same time.

So when you feel your anxiety spike, use your breath. It's a powerful tool to bring you back to the moment and break the cycle of stress.

3. Journaling: Clear the Mental Clutter

Here's another tool: get it out of your head. If your mind is cluttered with racing thoughts, write them down. Write out everything that's bothering you. Once the thoughts are on paper, they're no longer buzzing around in your head. You've externalized them.

Write down what's bothering you. What's stressing you out? What thoughts keep coming back? Then ask yourself, *Is this helpful?* Most of the time, it's not. You're just replaying the same narrative. Once you identify that, you can start shifting your mindset.

A Guru's Mental Discipline: Own Your Thoughts

Let me make one thing clear: this isn't about being "perfect" at quieting your mind. It's not about being some zen monk who never thinks a negative thought. It's about *mental discipline*. A guru has the discipline to notice the noise, shut it down, and replace it with what they want to focus on. They don't let their thoughts run the show. They are the *masters* of their mind.

Action Plan: Start using these tools every single day. Don't wait for a crisis to hit before you try them. Practice saying "Stop" when your thoughts run wild. Take a moment to breathe deeply. Write down your anxious thoughts, and then question them. Slowly, you'll build the mental discipline you need to stay calm when the world tries to pull you apart.

Here's the bottom line: if you don't quiet your mind, you'll never be in control. It's not enough to just manage your external circumstances—you need to manage your internal state. The noise in your head is a direct reflection of how much control you have over your thoughts and emotions.

If you're ready to become a Modern Guru, it's time to quiet that noise and get your mind working for you, not against you.

You control your mind. **Now act like it.**

Part 3: The Guru's Mental Discipline

———

Get this straight: **A true guru is not a guru because of what they know.** They're a guru because of how they *respond*—or, more accurately, how they *don't respond*. In the chaos of life, where everyone is losing their minds, the guru stands still. The guru is unshaken, unmovable, like a rock in a storm. It's not that the guru never faces challenges or feels emotions—they do. They're human. But what separates them from the rest of us is **their discipline.** They don't let their emotions or thoughts run the show. They control them. And if you want to think like a guru, you'd better start doing the same.

This isn't about living in a peaceful monastery where the only sound is the rustling of leaves. We live in a world that's *loud*. Full of distractions, pressures, stress. But this is exactly where the guru shines. **They have mastered the art of staying calm in the chaos.** That's the *mental discipline* we're talking about.

If you're ready to stop being dragged around by your emotions, your stress, your thoughts, then buckle up. This chapter is going to show you how to build the mental discipline that will change your life.

How a Guru Maintains Calmness Amidst Chaos

Think about the last time everything went sideways in your life. Maybe it was work stress. Maybe a relationship blew up. Maybe you just woke up feeling *off*. In those moments, the mind races. Your body tenses up. Your thoughts flood in, one after another, each one fueling the fire. It's easy to get swept up in that current of chaos.

Now picture this: **A guru walking into the middle of that storm.** The winds are howling, the waves are crashing. But the guru is as calm as a still lake. They're not ignoring the storm. They're not pretending it isn't there. They are simply not letting it *consume* them.

Here's the secret: The guru knows how to maintain inner calm because they don't engage with every thought, every feeling, every external noise. They know that **peace is a choice**. It's not something that "happens" to you. It's something you *choose*—again and again. The storm might rage around you, but you don't have to let it inside.

The guru is always in control of their mind. When something disruptive happens—someone criticizes them, they face a setback—they don't jump into the emotional spin cycle. They *pause*. They don't let their immediate reactions rule them. And here's the kicker: **They don't take it personally.**

The Guru's Secret to Staying Calm

How do they do this? Simple: they've mastered **mental discipline**. They train their minds just like an athlete trains their body. And just like you can't be a top athlete without pushing yourself, you can't be mentally disciplined without *practice*.

Think about it: when you practice, you get better. But only if you stick with it. And that's exactly what a guru does with their mind. **They practice mental discipline, every day, whether they feel like it or not.**

The moment you let your mind wander into reactions—whether it's anger, fear, or frustration—you've lost control. You've allowed your emotions to hijack your thinking. But a guru is always aware of what's happening inside them. They catch the reaction before it takes hold, and they choose to act, not react. They don't let life decide how they feel. They take that power back.

Practical Tools for Practicing Mental Discipline

Now, let's get to the real meat of this: *How do you practice mental discipline?* You're not going to become a guru overnight, but with the right tools and consistent effort, you'll start noticing the difference.

1. Mindfulness: The Foundation of Mental Discipline

Let's start with **mindfulness**—this is the bedrock of mental discipline. Without mindfulness, you're just a ship lost at sea, at the mercy of your emotions and thoughts. Mindfulness is the practice of being fully present in the moment, without judgment.

It's so simple, yet so hard. When you're mindful, you're aware of what's happening in your body and mind *without getting sucked into it*. You notice your thoughts, your feelings, and your reactions, but you don't let them control you.

Here's your challenge: Spend 10 minutes every morning sitting quietly. Focus on your breath. As you breathe in and out, just observe what comes up. Thoughts, feelings, sensations—they'll all float through your mind. Your job is not to engage with them, but simply to notice them. When a thought arises, don't chase it down. Don't argue with it. Just *let it go*. Focus back on your breath.

You'll be shocked at how difficult this is at first. Your mind will try to pull you into a million directions. That's okay. Don't judge yourself for getting distracted. Just keep coming back to your breath. Over time, this practice will help you catch your reactions and thoughts in real-time throughout the day. It's the first step in building true mental discipline.

2. Detachment: Letting Go of Attachment to Outcomes

Another key element of a guru's mental discipline is **detachment**. And by detachment, I don't mean *not caring* about anything. I mean learning how to let go of your attachment to specific outcomes. When you're attached to something, you give away your peace. Whether it's a relationship, a career goal, or a material possession, attachment ties you to a specific outcome, and if that outcome doesn't unfold the way you want it to, you lose your calm.

Here's an example: Imagine you've been working on a big project at work. You've poured your energy into it, sacrificed sleep, maybe even lost your temper a few times. You *want* the outcome to be perfect. Then, one day, your boss criticizes your work. What happens? Your calmness goes out the window. You feel defensive, hurt, angry—because you were *attached* to the outcome. You wanted validation.

The guru doesn't care about validation. They know the outcome is not in their control. What is in their control is their effort and their response. When you detach from the outcome, you free yourself from unnecessary stress. You become unstoppable, because no matter what happens, you're still standing tall.

3. Thought Awareness: Catching the Negative Patterns

Another tool for mental discipline is **thought awareness**. The guru constantly scans their mind for unproductive thought patterns. Are you stuck in a loop of negative thinking? Are you constantly comparing yourself to others? Are you fixating on things that didn't work out? Catch those thoughts early, before they spiral out of control.

Here's an exercise for you: **The 5-Second Rule.** When you catch yourself thinking negatively or overthinking a situation, count backward from 5. 5...4...3...2...1. This short-circuiting technique interrupts the flow of negative thinking. As soon as you hit "1," choose to redirect your thoughts. Think about something that makes you feel good. Focus on something positive, something within your control.

It's simple, but it's effective. The goal is to stop negative thoughts in their tracks before they run away with your peace.

Master Your Mind, Master Your Life

Listen up. You want to think like a guru? Then you have to be serious about your mental discipline. This isn't about feeling "good" all the time or avoiding discomfort. It's about developing the strength to stay calm in the storm. To rise above the chaos instead of being pulled under by it.

Your mind is your greatest asset, but only if you learn to control it. If you don't, it will control you. Mental discipline isn't a one-time thing. It's a daily practice. Start small, but stay consistent. The more you practice, the stronger your mind becomes.

Now, go out there and get to work. Don't wait for the perfect moment. Build your discipline. Quiet the noise. And become the calm in the chaos. The world doesn't need more people reacting to everything. It needs more people who can *lead* with their calmness, their wisdom, and their mental strength.

You're ready. Now get to it.

Part 4: Achieving Lasting Peace

———

Alright, enough with the theory. If you want lasting peace—peace that sticks with you even when the world is coming at you like a freight train—you're going to need more than just a good attitude. You need **strategy.** You need tools that **work.** This isn't about fluff or feel-good mantras; this is about real, scientifically-backed methods that you can put into action starting today. And let me tell you something: It's possible.

The ancient gurus weren't just meditating on mountaintops for the sake of it. They knew the mind could be trained, **shaped**, and **retrained.** Today, we call it **neuroplasticity**—the brain's ability to change itself in response to experience. And guess what? **You have the power to reshape your mind** in real-time.

Now let's break this down. **How do you cultivate lasting peace in the midst of chaos?** How do you make mental stillness a lifestyle, not a temporary state of mind? I'm going to show you exactly how to do it.

The Science Behind Mental Peace: Neuroplasticity and Mindfulness

If you're still stuck on the idea that peace of mind is something only a few lucky people are born with, you need to snap out of it. **Mental peace is a skill you develop.** The science behind it is rooted in something called neuroplasticity. It's the brain's ability to reorganize itself by forming new neural connections throughout your life. What does that mean? **It means that with the right practice, you can actually reshape your brain to become more peaceful.**

Here's the bottom line: Your brain is like a muscle. **The more you work it, the stronger it gets.** When you practice mindfulness, meditation, and other mental disciplines, you're literally rewiring your brain to respond with more calmness and less stress.

But let me give it to you straight: **It won't happen overnight. This takes consistent effort.** You're not going to walk out of your first meditation session feeling like the Dalai Lama. But after days, weeks, and months of practice, you'll start to notice a change. The things that used to stress you out—people cutting you off in traffic, bad news, or your boss's impossible demands—won't trigger you in the same way. The more you practice, the more you wire your brain to stay calm and composed.

Now, if you're wondering how mindfulness fits into all of this, let me break it down. **Mindfulness is the vehicle through which you shape your brain.** Mindfulness trains your brain to be aware of what's happening right now—without judgment. It stops the cycle of mental chatter, the automatic stress responses, and the endless loop of worries. Through mindfulness, you can break free from being the slave of your own mind.

Here's what we know: Studies have shown that consistent mindfulness practice can actually **increase grey matter** in the areas of the brain responsible for emotional regulation, self-awareness, and empathy. In other words, it makes your brain physically **better** at staying calm. So this isn't some new-age, wishful thinking; this is brain science. **You can literally train your brain to be more peaceful.**

How to Cultivate a Lifestyle that Supports Mental Stillness

Alright, now that we've got the science under our belt, let's talk about the practical side. It's all well and good to talk about peace of mind, but how do you make it stick? How do you build a lifestyle that supports mental stillness, especially when the world keeps throwing distractions at you?

1. Start Your Day with Intention

The first hour of your day sets the tone for everything. I'm not going to sugarcoat it—if you roll out of bed and immediately check your phone, let the news hit you, or get lost in your to-do list, you're already putting your mind on the back foot. **You have to take control of that first hour.** This is crucial. You want to start your day in a state of calm and focus, not chaos.

So, how do you do that? Simple: **Start with stillness.**

- **Wake up 10-15 minutes earlier than usual.**
- **Don't grab your phone.**
- Sit up in bed or in a chair, close your eyes, and take a few deep breaths. This isn't about zoning out—it's about reconnecting with the present moment.

This could be as simple as practicing a brief meditation or just breathing mindfully. It's not about being perfect—it's about setting a tone for your day. Do this every morning. Your mind will learn to associate the first moments of the day with calm.

1. **Eliminate Distractions (Or At Least Control Them)**

This is where most people fail. The world is filled with distractions. And if you let them, they will control your mind. But **you are not your distractions**. You control what you allow into your mind.

- **Set boundaries around technology.** Don't check your email every 5 minutes. Don't scroll mindlessly through social media. These things pull you out of the present moment and into a state of stress.
- **Turn off notifications**—this one is crucial. Your phone is a chaos machine. You don't need to be notified every time someone posts a picture or sends you a message.
- **Make space for silence.** If you're used to constant noise, whether it's the TV, music, or chatter, create moments of silence throughout the day. You don't need to be entertained 24/7. Silence recalibrates your mind.

The more you control your environment, the more you create space for peace. **You can't have stillness if you're constantly surrounded by noise.**

1. **Practice Mindfulness Throughout Your Day**

You can't just meditate for 10 minutes in the morning and then expect peace to last all day. **Peace of mind is a practice.** You have to train your mind throughout the day to stay centered.

- **Mindfulness in Movement:** Whether you're walking, eating, or doing a task, bring your attention fully to what you're doing. Don't just go through the motions. **Be present.**
- **Mindful Breathing:** When you start to feel your stress levels rise, don't wait until you're about to snap. Stop. Breathe. Take a few deep, slow breaths. This simple act helps reset your nervous system.
- **Pause and Reflect:** When you're in the middle of a conversation or work task, take short pauses to check in with yourself. Notice your thoughts, your emotions, and your body. Are you getting tense? Are your thoughts spiraling? Recognizing this is the first step in bringing yourself back to calm.

1. **Exercise: Moving Your Body to Calm Your Mind**

This isn't just about looking good—it's about feeling good. Exercise releases endorphins, those feel-good chemicals in your brain that reduce stress. But more importantly, it helps you stay **in your body**, which pulls you out of your mind.

It doesn't matter if it's yoga, running, swimming, or weightlifting—find a form of exercise that you enjoy and make it part of your routine. Regular physical activity reduces stress hormones like cortisol and helps your brain stay balanced. **Exercise is like a reset button for your mind.**

The Bottom Line: You Can Have Lasting Peace, But It's Up to You

Here's the deal: **Peace is not something you wait for. It's something you create.** The world is going to keep being chaotic, but you don't have to be swept up in it. Through neuroplasticity, mindfulness, and the right lifestyle choices, you can cultivate lasting peace. But it's up to you to put the work in.

Start with the basics: set your day up for success, eliminate distractions, practice mindfulness, and get your body moving. That's the foundation.

Here's your challenge: **Practice one of these steps each day for the next 30 days.** Don't skip, don't cheat, don't make excuses. Build a life of mental stillness, one choice at a time. When you're done, come back and tell me how much better you feel.

Peace is yours for the taking. But you've got to choose it, every single day. Now, get to work.

Chapter 2: Living in the Present Moment: The Guru's Power of Now

Part 1: The Trap of Time: Past, Present, and Future

———

Let me break it down for you right now: **You are living in the past or the future, and it's costing you everything.** That's the cold, hard truth. Your mind is either stuck replaying something you did wrong yesterday or worrying about what could go wrong tomorrow. But guess what? **That's not life.** That's a **distraction.** You've bought into the biggest illusion of them all: **time.**

It's time for you to get real. Right now. The past is gone. The future hasn't happened yet. All you've got is the present—**this moment.** But the problem is, most people don't know how to stay here. They've been trained to think they need to constantly chase what happened before or what's coming next. And let me tell you, it's **destroying you.** You're missing out on the only thing that's real: **the now.**

In this chapter, we're going to talk about the trap of time—the past and future—and why it's keeping you from the peace and power you're seeking. You want the mind of a guru? Then you need to learn how to live **in the present moment.** And I'm going to show you exactly how to do it.

The Cultural Obsession with the Past and Future

Walk into any conversation, and what do you hear? "Remember when..." "I'm thinking about what's next..." The past and future are constantly being replayed like a bad movie. And here's the kicker: **Most of the time, it's all a story we tell ourselves.** That "good ol' days" memory? It's not the truth—it's just a bunch of mental images. The future? It doesn't exist. **You can't predict it.** You can only control this moment. But the culture we live in is obsessed with the past and future. The media feeds you history lessons, politicians push for a "better tomorrow," and social media keeps you trapped in yesterday's posts and tomorrow's trends.

People get wrapped up in **regret** over the past—replaying every decision, every mistake, every missed opportunity. Then they dive into **anxiety** over the future—what might go wrong, what they might not achieve, what could happen next. This constant flipping between regret and worry takes its toll. It pulls you away from the only place where real power lives: the **present.**

And don't think you're immune to this. You think you're different? You're not. Everyone does it. You dwell on old mistakes, beating yourself up over things that are **gone**. You obsess over the future, worrying about things that haven't happened yet. You get lost in **time**, as if the past and future are more important than the reality of now.

But here's the truth: You can't change the past, and you can't control the future. **All you've got is this moment.**

How the Mind Dwells in the Past and Future, Robbing Us of the Present

Here's the problem: your mind is a **wild animal**. It jumps from one thing to the next, and it's usually jumping between the past and the future. It's constantly revisiting old wounds, old arguments, or old regrets, or it's running simulations of what might happen next. The **present**? That's boring, right? That's not exciting. That doesn't make you feel alive. Wrong.

The real reason your mind dwells in the past or future is because it feels safe there. The present is where **uncertainty** lives. It's where real life happens. It's where you have to make real decisions. The past is something you know, something you can control with your memory. The future is something you can control with your imagination. But the present is different. It demands that you show up. **Fully.**

Think about it. When was the last time you were fully present in a conversation? When you weren't thinking about what to say next, or how that person might perceive you? When was the last time you did something—anything—without mentally checking out? This is where the magic happens, folks. When you are completely immersed in what's happening right now, you are not distracted by what's already happened or what might happen next.

Let me tell you a personal story to make this clear. A few years ago, I was living in a state of constant mental **distraction.** I was constantly ruminating on the mistakes I'd made, decisions I'd regretted, relationships I had screwed up. I was also deeply worried about what was coming—what was going to happen in my career, with my family, with the world. I thought that if I could just solve these problems, if I could just fix what happened before and control what was coming, everything would be okay.

But guess what? **I was wrong.** Nothing I did could change the past. And no amount of worry about the future did anything to actually prepare me for what came next. It took me a long time to wake up to this truth: the more I obsessed over the past and future, the less I actually **lived.**

I'll give it to you straight: **Living in the past and future is a form of escape.** It's easier to dwell on what's gone wrong than to face what's happening right now. It's easier to worry about tomorrow than to take responsibility for what you can do today. But here's the deal—you'll never be in control of your life until you stop running from the present.

The Guru's Approach: Mastering the Present

So, what does it take to live in the present moment like a **guru**? How do you stop being pulled around by the past and the future? Simple: **You start practicing awareness.**

A true guru doesn't get lost in time. They're not running from their past, and they're not obsessing about the future. They are **masters** of the present. They know that life only exists right now. So they learn to tune into this moment—the only place where real life is happening.

Here's how you can start mastering the present:

1. Awareness is Your First Tool.

The first step is awareness. Catch yourself when you start to drift off into past memories or future scenarios. You've got to develop the **self-awareness** to know when you're lost in thought. When you catch yourself, stop. Take a breath. Refocus on what's happening right now. **Be here.** This takes practice, but eventually, you'll start to catch yourself sooner. You'll develop a muscle for the present moment.

2. Refocus on Your Senses.

The best way to snap out of mental time travel is to reconnect with your senses. Touch something. Look around and really notice your surroundings. Feel your feet on the ground. Listen to the sounds around you. **Engage with the present** by reconnecting with your body and the world around you.

3. Embrace the Discomfort of the Present.

Living in the present is not always comfortable. The mind likes to escape. But **discomfort is where growth happens.** If you find yourself uncomfortable with what's happening now, don't run. Sit with it. Challenge yourself to stay present, even when it feels easier to retreat into the past or future. The more you practice this, the more you build your mental **resilience.**

4. Shift Your Mindset: It's Not About Controlling Time—It's About Letting Go.

Finally, shift your mindset. Stop trying to **control** time. You don't own the past, and the future isn't yours to command. The only thing you have is **now.** And that's enough. By letting go of the need to control, you start to free yourself from the shackles of time.

Live Now or Miss Life

Here's the deal: if you don't learn to live in the present, you're **missing** your life. The past is over. The future isn't here yet. The only time you have is **right now.** This is it. **This moment is all you've got.**

The question is: will you show up for it? Will you stop running from the past and future? Will you stop letting time rob you of the only thing that's real?

It's time to wake up. Stop being a slave to the past and future. Start living in the present. If you do that, you'll discover a whole new world—a world of peace, of power, of clarity. **The only place where life happens is right here, right now.** It's your choice whether you're going to show up for it.

Part 2: Mastering Presence

Listen up. If you want to live like a guru—if you want the calm, the clarity, the **focus**—then **presence** is your key. But here's the problem: most people don't know what presence really means. They think it's about being in the moment once in a while. Wrong. Presence is not a passive state you visit; it's an **active practice**. It's not something you "try" to do when you're in the mood. **It's something you do all the time.** Right now, right here, in everything you do. You want to step into the mind of a modern guru? Then you need to understand how to master the art of **presence**—to be fully in each moment, without distraction, without hesitation, and without hesitation.

So let me get straight to it: **Presence is everything. Presence is power.** It's what separates those who drift through life like zombies and those who are fully alive.

The Techniques Used by Modern Gurus to Stay Fully Present

Now, you might be thinking, "That sounds good, but how do I actually do that?" Well, first off, it's not about some magical switch you flip. **Presence is a skill you develop.** You practice it. The gurus—whether it's a monk, a Zen master, or a spiritual teacher—they didn't just wake up one day and decide to be present. They worked at it. They built the muscle of awareness, just like you build any muscle.

Let me break it down for you.

1. The Power of the Breath

The first step to mastering presence? The breath. Every guru knows it. You know why? **Breathing is the most fundamental anchor** you have to the present moment. Try it right now. Take a slow, deep breath. Feel the air fill your lungs. Let it out. Pay attention. **Just breathe.** Do you notice that feeling of being **here**? That's the power of the breath. It's your immediate link to now.

Now, this isn't just about breathing as a quick fix when you're stressed. This is about **creating a habit** of breath awareness throughout the day. Modern gurus do it all the time. Whether they're sitting in meditation or walking down the street, they are *conscious* of their breath. It's an anchor, and it pulls them back to the present. So here's what you do: whenever you find yourself distracted, whenever you find your mind wandering, **pause**. Breathe. **Return** your awareness to the rhythm of your breath. It sounds simple, but it's one of the most powerful techniques for staying present.

2. Mindfulness in the Mundane

The second technique? Mindfulness. But not the kind you've heard of in some trendy article about "mindful eating" or "mindful walking." This isn't just about paying attention when you're doing something fancy or "spiritual." **This is about being mindful in every damn thing you do**. Modern gurus don't just show up for their "special" moments; they show up for **every single moment**.

When you're eating, **be present** with every bite. When you're walking, **be present** with every step. When you're washing the dishes, don't let your mind drift to what happened earlier or what's coming later. Be present with the water, the soap, the feel of the dish in your hand. The goal is to infuse presence into the most mundane, boring moments of your day. You'll be shocked at how much life opens up when you commit to mindfulness in the smallest tasks.

Here's an exercise for you: **Pick one task today that you usually do on autopilot**—washing your hands, making your coffee, brushing your teeth—and do it **mindfully**. Pay attention to every single detail. The taste, the sound, the texture. Engage your senses completely. Do this, and you'll start realizing how much you miss when you're operating on auto-pilot.

3. Body Awareness and Embodiment

If you're not aware of your body, you're not present. Period. The body is the vessel through which you experience life, and if you're not **aware** of how it feels, then you're not **here**. Modern gurus practice what's called **embodiment**. It means paying attention to the sensations in your body at all times. How does your posture feel right now? Is there tension in your shoulders? Are you holding your breath? How are your feet pressing against the floor?

Gurus use body awareness to stay grounded in the present moment. And guess what? You can, too. If you find yourself getting distracted or anxious, **check in with your body.** Feel your feet on the ground. Relax your shoulders. Take a few deep breaths and feel your body settle into the moment.

The Practice of Mindfulness and Embodiment in Daily Life

I'm going to give you a few specific steps to bring this into your life. You want to become a master of presence? Then start right now. This is how you do it.

Step 1: Set Intentions to Be Present

You have to make a decision to be present. It's not going to just happen by accident. Set a clear intention for the day: **"I'm going to show up in each moment today."** Say it out loud. Declare it. Tell yourself that you are going to live in the now. Put your phone down, turn off distractions, and focus.

Step 2: Start Small: Mindful Moments

You're not going to suddenly start living in the present all day, every day. It's a practice. Start small. Pick 3-5 moments throughout the day where you can be fully present. Could be while drinking your morning coffee. Could be while driving. Could be when you're talking to someone. **Choose moments when you can give your full attention to the experience.** Nothing else matters for those few minutes. Your only job is to be fully there. Practice this.

Step 3: Use Your Body to Bring You Back

When you get distracted (and you will—it's normal), bring yourself back to the present by checking in with your body. Feel your feet on the ground. Roll your shoulders back. Relax your jaw. Feel the tension melt away as you come back to your breath. **Use your body to anchor yourself in the present moment.** It's like hitting the reset button on your mental state.

Step 4: Turn Everyday Activities Into Mindfulness Practices

You don't need a special time or a fancy meditation cushion to practice mindfulness. Every moment can be an opportunity to be present. **Turn your daily routine into your mindfulness practice.** Walking to the store? That's an opportunity to be present. Washing dishes? That's an opportunity to be present. Drinking water? Same thing. Every task is an opportunity to return your focus to the now. If you're walking to the mailbox, focus on the feeling of your feet on the ground, the temperature of the air, the sounds around you. **That's mindfulness.**

Step 5: Practice Non-Resistance

One of the most powerful aspects of mastering presence is learning not to resist whatever comes up. Here's the thing: the present moment doesn't always feel easy. Maybe you're stuck in traffic. Maybe your body is sore. Maybe there's noise around you. **Don't resist.** Instead of fighting what's happening, learn to fully accept it. The moment is what it is. Embrace it. If you're stuck in traffic, embrace the stillness. If you're tired, embrace the fatigue. The guru doesn't fight what is; they surrender to it. That's how they stay present—by accepting life as it unfolds.

Show Up for Your Life

Let me hit you with the bottom line: **You can't be present if you're not showing up.** Modern gurus are able to stay present because they show up for their lives—**fully.** They don't hide from the discomforts of the present moment, and they don't run to the past or future for comfort. They are fully engaged in what is happening **right now. That's your challenge, too.**

You don't need to wait for a perfect moment. You don't need to wait until you "feel like it." Presence is something you choose to practice, moment by moment. **Show up for your life**—right now. And remember, presence isn't a one-time thing. It's something you do **every day**. Stay aware. Stay mindful. Stay in your body. And when you catch yourself slipping into the past or the future, use your breath to bring you back.

The guru's power is in their ability to stay **here**—in the now. So, get to it. Show up. Live now.

Part 3: Embracing Impermanence

———

Let me make this clear: **nothing lasts forever.** Your youth, your job, your relationships, your body—all of it's temporary. The good stuff, the bad stuff, it's all going to pass. That's a fact. **If you want to master the mind of a guru**, you need to understand and accept this truth. **Embrace impermanence.** Because here's the deal: resisting it will only make you miserable.

But most people, they fight it. They try to hold onto things—people, situations, emotions—that aren't meant to last. They cling to what's comfortable. They want things to stay the same, even when deep down they know everything is changing. So they end up stressed, anxious, and out of sync with the natural flow of life. **You have two choices: you can fight impermanence, or you can flow with it.** One will lead to suffering. The other will lead to peace. Choose wisely.

The Power of Accepting the Temporary Nature of All Things

Let's get real for a second. Every day, you're watching things change. **You wake up, and the world around you is different**—a little older, a little wiser, a little more worn. Your body's changing, too. Your thoughts, your desires, they shift as you go through life. Relationships evolve. Seasons change. Even your feelings—your emotions—are constantly fluctuating. **The only thing that stays constant is change itself.** And if you're fighting it, you're fighting life. You're swimming upstream.

The power of embracing impermanence is that it frees you from this constant tension. It liberates you from the need to control everything. **When you accept the temporary nature of all things, you stop holding onto things that aren't meant to stay.** You can enjoy what you have, without the fear of losing it. That's the secret. Most people are afraid of losing what they have. They hoard experiences, relationships, material things, because they fear that when it's gone, they'll be left with nothing. But that's a lie. **What you fear losing is just the illusion of permanence.**

A guru knows that nothing is permanent, and that's why they don't hold on too tightly. They experience life fully, but they don't cling to any of it. Think of it this way: **life is like a river.** You're floating along in a boat, and the river is constantly flowing, carrying you forward. You can't stop it. You can't hold onto the water. But you can enjoy the ride. When you embrace the flow, you don't fight the current. You **let go.**

Learning to Flow with Life Rather Than Resist It

The core of this idea is simple: **stop resisting life.** Life is going to do its thing—people will come and go, your job will change, your health will fluctuate, your dreams may evolve. So stop resisting that. Instead, learn to flow with it. You don't control the flow of the river. You don't control the tide. But you can control **how you ride it.**

This is exactly how a guru handles the chaos of life. When something changes—good or bad—they don't lose their cool. They don't try to hold onto the good stuff, and they don't run from the bad stuff. **They accept what is, and they adapt.**

Look at it like this: You're on a road trip. Your car is going to encounter potholes, speed bumps, detours. **You can either scream at the potholes and curse the detours, or you can keep your hands on the wheel and keep driving.** It's that simple. The road will twist and turn, but if you keep fighting it, you're going to crash. If you relax and navigate it, you'll get where you're going.

The Art of Detachment

This is where you need to start practicing **detachment**. And before you get all defensive, let me be clear: detachment doesn't mean you stop caring. It doesn't mean you become cold or indifferent. It means you **don't let your happiness depend on something outside of you.** You enjoy life fully, but you don't become attached to it. You **detach** from the idea that things should stay the same. You let go of the illusion that you can control everything.

Detachment is the power to enjoy your experiences without the fear of losing them. You love your job, your relationships, your home—**but you don't tie your identity to them**. When you detach, you stop relying on these external factors for your sense of worth. You realize that **your true peace comes from within**, not from the outside world.

To practice detachment, you need to start by recognizing when you're getting too attached to something—whether it's a material possession, a relationship, or even an outcome you're hoping for. If you're attached to something, you're creating tension. **You're setting yourself up for disappointment when that thing inevitably changes or disappears.**

Ask yourself: **What am I attached to? Why does it matter so much? Can I still feel whole if it's gone?**

The Role of Impermanence in Reducing Fear and Anxiety

Most people are **afraid** of change. They fear the unknown. They fear the loss of what they have. But here's the truth: fear is only there because you're clinging to things that aren't meant to last. **The more you try to control life, the more you're going to fear losing control.**

A guru doesn't fear change because they've already accepted that everything is temporary. They **flow with life** rather than resisting it. They don't fear loss because they know that when one door closes, another will open. **They trust in the impermanence of things**—because that trust brings them peace. They don't get upset when things change; they **embrace it**. It's like the seasons. Winter comes, but so does spring. **Change is inevitable, but it's not the end of the world.**

So, if you want to conquer fear and anxiety, you need to stop resisting change. **Let go** of your attachment to the idea of permanence. **Learn to ride the wave of life instead of drowning in it.** And when something difficult comes up—whether it's a loss, a setback, or a challenge—recognize that it's temporary. This too shall pass.

The Guru's Mindset: Trusting the Flow

Let me give it to you straight: **The guru doesn't try to hold on to anything.** They're not attached to their possessions, their appearance, their accomplishments, or even their relationships. They are not *immune* to loss, but they know how to deal with it. They don't panic. They don't resist. They understand that everything in life is **temporary**.

They **trust the flow** of life. They know that whatever happens—whether it's good or bad—it's part of the natural order. And if they lose something or someone, they **don't see it as the end**. They see it as part of the bigger picture. They know that life is constantly unfolding, constantly changing. **The universe is moving in its own way**, and they don't fight it.

You need to trust the flow too. **Life is not something you need to control**. It's something you need to experience fully. Flow with it. Surrender to it. If you fight change, you'll waste your energy. But if you trust the flow, you'll find peace. **You'll find freedom.**

Action Steps to Embrace Impermanence

- **Identify What You're Holding Onto:** What are you clinging to in your life that's creating tension? Is it a relationship, a job, a possession, or even an idea of how things should be? Recognize that nothing is permanent.
- **Practice Detachment:** Start with small things. Let go of the need to control everything. Detach your happiness from external factors. Stop seeking validation from others.
- **Let Go of Fear:** Every time you feel fear of losing something, remind yourself: **it's temporary.** It's not the end. Change is inevitable, but so is growth.
- **Embrace the Flow:** Learn to accept life as it comes. Trust that even when things seem difficult, it's just part of the cycle.

Everything passes. Trust the flow, and stop trying to control it.

Live Fully in the Now

The bottom line: if you want peace, you need to **embrace impermanence**. Stop fighting life. **Flow with it.** Let go of the need to control everything. Accept that everything—*and everyone*—is temporary. And when you accept this, you'll find a deep sense of peace. **That's how the guru lives**—fully present, not attached to anything, trusting in the flow of life. Now, get to it.

Part 4: The Gift of Now

Let's cut through the crap—**the present moment is all you've got.** Everything else is either a memory or an imagination. The past is gone, the future hasn't happened yet, and the only real thing in your life right now is this breath you're taking. **Everything else is an illusion.** Get over the fantasy that you can control anything outside of the present moment.

You think you can shape the future or undo the past? Good luck with that. You can't. But what you **can** do, right now, is choose how you engage with the present moment. That's the gift. **That's the power.** When you choose to live in the here and now, you stop wasting energy on things that don't matter, and you start tapping into the real power that comes from being fully engaged with life as it is, **right now.**

A guru understands this better than anyone. The guru is not some enlightened being living in the clouds. The guru is a person who knows how to live **fully** in the present moment, no matter what's going on around them. They're not looking for peace somewhere in the future or regretting the past—they're rooted in the present, and that's where their strength comes from. If you want that strength, you need to understand **why the present moment is the most powerful place to be.**

How Embracing the Present Moment Creates Peace and Personal Power

Let me make this as blunt as possible—**when you live in the present moment, you reclaim your power.** Why? Because when you're stuck in the past, you're constantly rehashing old memories, reliving past mistakes, and refeeding old wounds. That keeps you stuck, and you lose your power in the process. You're not here, you're not now, you're somewhere else—wallowing in regret or nostalgia.

When you're obsessed with the future, you're worried, anxious, and overwhelmed. You're trying to control what you can't. You're anxious about things that haven't even happened yet. But guess what? **The future doesn't exist yet.** It's a projection. It's all in your head. So, when you live in the future, you're not in control—you're just stuck in a cycle of anxiety.

But when you're in the present, **you take control.** You stop playing the "what if" game. You stop clinging to the past, and you stop obsessing over the future. **You take your power back.** This is where peace begins. The present moment is the only place where you can actually make a change. Not in the past, not in the future—**only in the now.**

I'll give you an example. Think of a time when you've been really engaged in something—like a conversation, or a task, or even just sitting quietly and enjoying a moment of stillness. When you're truly immersed in that experience, you're not thinking about your to-do list. You're not thinking about what someone said to you last week. **You're completely present**, and in that moment, there is no tension, no anxiety, no fear. There's just peace.

That's the power of now. The more you embrace the present, the more power you have to create change in your life. The more you're able to be in the moment, the less you'll be weighed down by the past or pulled into the future.

Practical Exercises to Anchor Yourself in the Present

Now, let's talk about how to do this. Because this isn't some abstract idea. You don't just think about living in the present moment. **You practice it.** It's like a muscle—you've got to build it.

Here are a few practical ways to start anchoring yourself in the present:

1. Focus on Your Breath

Sounds simple, but don't overlook this. The breath is the quickest way to bring yourself back to the present moment. Try this: Sit down, close your eyes, and take a deep breath in. Hold it for a second, and then exhale slowly.

Focus on how the air feels entering your body, filling your lungs, and then leaving. **Every breath is a moment.**

You can do this anytime—before a meeting, during a stressful situation, or when you're feeling overwhelmed. **When you focus on your breath**, you immediately pull yourself into the present. The more you do this, the more you train your mind to stop jumping into the past or future. It's that simple.

2. Engage Your Senses

This is a great way to ground yourself when your mind starts to wander. Stop for a moment and engage your senses. **What can you hear?** Really listen. What can you see? What do you smell, taste, or feel? Take a moment to take in the present moment with your senses. **This brings you out of your head and into your body.**

It's impossible to worry about the future or dwell on the past when you're fully engaged with the world around you. Use your senses to connect with the here and now.

3. Mindful Walking

Walking is one of the easiest ways to practice presence. But don't just walk mindlessly like most people do—**pay attention to every step**. Feel the ground under your feet. Notice the movement of your body as you walk. Breathe with each step.

If your mind starts to wander, simply bring it back to the sensation of walking. Notice the rhythm of your feet hitting the ground. This keeps you anchored in the present moment, and before you know it, you'll be more aware of your surroundings, of your body, and of your thoughts.

4. Single-Tasking

Stop multitasking. It's a trap. When you're juggling multiple things at once, you're splitting your attention, and that's a surefire way to pull yourself out of the present moment. Instead, focus on one task at a time. **Give your**

full attention to whatever you're doing—whether it's eating, working, or having a conversation.

If you catch yourself thinking about something else, gently bring your attention back to the task at hand. **Focus on the now**, and the more you do this, the more you'll begin to experience the power of presence.

5. Practice Gratitude

Another powerful tool for staying in the present is gratitude. When you feel yourself drifting into worry or regret, take a moment to think about what you're grateful for in the here and now. What do you have right now that is good? Your health, your family, your ability to read this book—whatever it is, **acknowledge it.**

Gratitude is a reminder that the present moment is enough. It pulls you away from the scarcity mindset that often dominates our thinking, and it reconnects you with the abundance that already exists in the here and now.

The Takeaway: The Power of Now Is in Your Hands

Here's the deal: **you have a choice.** You can keep living in the past, stewing over old wounds, or you can keep worrying about the future and letting anxiety run your life. Or you can wake up to the truth—that the only thing that's real is the present moment. And when you embrace that, you reclaim your power.

The gift of now is yours to claim. The present moment holds the power to heal, to transform, to create. It's the only place where real change can happen. So stop wasting time. Stop waiting for the right moment. **The right moment is now.**

The guru lives in the present. They don't wait for the perfect time, they don't wish for the past, and they don't fear the future. They are here. Now. **That's where the power is.**

Now, **go practice it.** It's time to stop making excuses. If you want peace, if you want power, **the time is now.**

Chapter 3: The Power of Awareness: Understanding Your Mind and Emotions

Part 1: The Guru's Awareness

———

Let's get this straight: **Awareness is everything.** There's no transformation without awareness. No true change, no enlightenment, no peace. If you're not aware of what's happening in your mind, your emotions, and your environment, you're just drifting. Reacting. **You're a victim of life.** The first step in mastering your life is understanding how awareness operates.

If you want to think like a guru, if you want to live like a guru, you have to **wake up**—and I mean really wake up. Most people are sleepwalking through life. They're unaware of their thoughts, their emotional triggers, and the patterns that control their every move. And let me tell you—**that's where the pain is born.**

A guru isn't just some zen-like figure who meditates in a cave. The guru is anyone who has learned to turn on their awareness and see things as they truly are, not through the fog of their habitual mind. The guru sees clearly. The guru is aware. And that awareness is the key to real, lasting transformation.

If you're serious about change, if you're ready to step up, this chapter is going to force you to take a hard look at the way you've been living. **You've been living asleep. It's time to wake up.**

Understanding How Awareness Is the Gateway to True Transformation

Transformation doesn't happen in the future. It happens right now. **It happens when you choose to wake up and look at things as they are, without the filters of your past, your beliefs, or your emotions.**

Most people move through life like zombies. They act on impulse, react to situations, and let their emotions control them. They don't stop to ask themselves, "Why do I feel this way? Why am I thinking this thought? What's going on underneath the surface?" They let life happen to them. They're just **reacting**.

But here's the thing: **If you don't change your awareness, you can't change anything**. Awareness is the starting point. Once you become aware of how your mind works—how it creates patterns, attachments, and judgments—you unlock the door to real transformation.

The guru knows this truth. They know that **change begins when you see things clearly**. They observe their thoughts and emotions without being controlled by them. They don't let their reactions dictate their actions. They **choose** how they respond, not from the emotional reactions of the past but from the clarity of conscious awareness.

You're not going to get the results you want in life until you take full ownership of your awareness. This means **watching yourself**. Not judging yourself, but simply noticing. The more you observe, the more you begin to separate yourself from your emotions, thoughts, and patterns. You become the **watcher**, not the participant. This is the gateway to personal freedom.

The Difference Between Reactive and Conscious Awareness

Here's where most people get tripped up: **They confuse reactive awareness with conscious awareness.** You see, reactive awareness is the default setting for most people. It's how you react when you're triggered—when someone cuts you off in traffic, when your boss criticizes you, when your partner does something annoying. **Your emotions take the wheel**, and you're just along for the ride.

You snap. You shout. You sulk. You get defensive. **You react.**

That's reactive awareness, and it's rooted in habit, fear, and past conditioning. It's the kind of awareness that keeps you trapped in cycles of frustration, resentment, and anxiety. It's automatic. It's **reactive.** You don't even notice it until it's too late. And before you know it, you've acted out of impulse, and you're left dealing with the consequences.

Conscious awareness, on the other hand, is different. Conscious awareness is the ability to step back and observe your thoughts, emotions, and actions without being swept away by them. It's a deliberate, mindful attention to the present moment. You **notice** your thoughts and feelings without judgment. You don't identify with them—you **witness** them. You understand that **thoughts are not facts** and emotions are not commands.

Conscious awareness is a decision. It's the ability to **choose your response** instead of just reacting. It's the difference between being a puppet to your emotions and being the master of your own actions. You're not stuck in patterns; you're free to choose how you engage with life.

Let's break this down with an example:

Imagine you're in a meeting, and someone criticizes your work. Your old, reactive awareness might kick in, and you immediately get defensive. You want to argue. You might even feel embarrassed or angry. **Your thoughts and emotions take control,** and you're immediately swept up in them.

Now, let's say you've cultivated conscious awareness. You feel the initial rush of anger or embarrassment, but instead of reacting immediately, you take a breath. You **pause,** and you **witness** your emotions. You don't identify with them. Instead of lashing out, you acknowledge how you feel, but you don't let those feelings dictate your actions. You stay grounded, take a moment to collect yourself, and respond calmly.

In that moment, you've just chosen a path of conscious awareness over reactive awareness. You've just broken a pattern. And that's how real transformation happens. **It's about interrupting the automatic reaction and choosing a new response.**

How to Cultivate Conscious Awareness

Now, let's get down to business. You've got to develop this conscious awareness, or nothing will change. It's like any skill—you have to practice it.

Here are some concrete steps to help you develop conscious awareness:

1. Start by Observing Your Thoughts

You don't have to control your thoughts or push them away. Just watch them. When you sit down to meditate or even when you're just going about your day, notice your thoughts. What are you thinking? Where do your thoughts go? How do they shape your emotions?

Don't get attached to any thought. **Just notice it.** The more you observe, the less control those thoughts will have over you. You'll begin to see them for what they are—**just thoughts**, not the truth.

2. Observe Your Emotions

Start noticing your emotional reactions. When something triggers you—whether it's a comment, a situation, or a person—pause and notice how you feel. Where do you feel it in your body? What emotion is present? **Just feel it, don't react to it.**

This is an important practice because emotions are often unconscious. They run the show unless you're paying attention. When you start observing your emotions, you begin to separate your true self from your emotional reactions.

3. Pause and Breathe

The next time you're about to react—whether it's to a person, a situation, or even an internal thought—pause. **Take a deep breath.** This moment of stillness creates a gap between stimulus and response. It allows you to make a conscious choice instead of reacting mindlessly.

This is where transformation happens: in the pause. That's when you decide how you'll respond, not from the past, but from awareness.

4. Journal Your Observations

Sometimes, your mind can be a jumble of thoughts and feelings. Writing them down helps you clarify your awareness. Spend five minutes a day journaling about what you noticed in your mind, body, and emotions that day. You'll start to see patterns, and when you become aware of those patterns, you have the power to change them.

The Takeaway: Awareness Is Your Superpower

Awareness is the key to everything. **Without it, you're just a puppet of your thoughts and emotions.** With it, you become the master of your mind. **The power of awareness is in your hands.** You have the ability to change, to break patterns, and to transform your life—but only if you start by waking up.

If you're serious about living like a modern guru, it starts with this: **Choose conscious awareness.** Notice your thoughts, feel your emotions, and decide how to respond. The more you do this, the more you will live with intention, clarity, and purpose.

Now get to work. Start observing. Start waking up. **It's time to break the cycle and take back control.**

Part 2: Emotional Mastery

———

Let's be brutally honest: **Your emotions are running the show.** Most of the time, you're not in control. Your anger, your fear, your frustration — they call the shots. But here's the hard truth: **Emotions aren't your problem. The real problem is that you're letting them control you.**

You want to think like a modern guru? It starts here. **Emotional mastery.** If you can't control your emotions, you're going to be a slave to them. If you don't recognize your emotional patterns, they'll dictate your choices, your relationships, and your peace of mind.

A guru isn't some passive observer to life. A guru doesn't get pushed around by their emotions. They're **aware** of their emotions, but they don't get hijacked by them. They've learned how to observe, understand, and ultimately **regulate** their emotional responses.

And I'm going to teach you to do the same. Because until you've mastered your emotions, you can't claim mastery over anything else.

Recognizing and Processing Emotions: Don't Let Them Control You

Most people have no idea what's going on with their emotions. They feel something, they act on it, and then they wonder why they've made a mess of things. **You've got to stop running from your emotions.**

Step one: Recognize them. Before you can process an emotion, you've got to **name it**. Anger, fear, jealousy, sadness—whatever it is, get clear on it. Stop pretending you don't feel it. Denial is a trap, and it's a trap that keeps you stuck. When you feel an emotion rise, don't avoid it, don't ignore it, and don't stuff it down. Recognize it.

If you feel angry, don't tell yourself, "I'm fine." Don't pretend like it's not happening. **Call it what it is.** You're angry. And that's okay. But recognizing the emotion is just the beginning.

Step two: Don't react. The next step is to not react to it. The emotional reaction is an automatic response, a reflex. But it doesn't have to control you. You feel angry? Fine. But that doesn't mean you have to yell or slam the door. You feel afraid? Okay. But that doesn't mean you have to freeze up or avoid the situation.

This is where most people fail. They feel an emotion, and immediately, they react. It's like a knee-jerk reflex. They've trained themselves to react out of habit, out of emotional programming. This is where you break the pattern.

The modern guru's approach is this: **Don't react to your emotions. Respond to them with awareness.** You've got to slow down. Take a breath. Let the initial wave of emotion pass. Then, consciously choose how to engage with that emotion.

Step three: Process the emotion. When you're able to recognize and pause, you're in a position to process. Emotions aren't meant to be avoided or suppressed. They're meant to be understood. They're signals. But you've got to ask yourself: *Why am I feeling this way?*

For example, if you're feeling anger, instead of just lashing out, ask yourself, **Why am I angry?** What is it about the situation that triggered this emotion? Is it your pride? A sense of injustice? Unmet expectations?

By diving into the root cause of the emotion, you start to understand its purpose. Anger, for instance, often signals a violation of your boundaries. Fear may point to a lack of control or an unmet need for safety. By digging deeper, you learn what the emotion is trying to tell you, and then you can decide how to respond effectively.

The Guru's Approach to Emotional Intelligence and Self-Regulation

Let's break it down: emotional intelligence is your ability to **recognize, understand, and manage your emotions**. It's a skill, not an innate gift. **You can develop it.** But it takes practice, patience, and consistency.

Here's the guru's approach to emotional mastery:

1. **Awareness of Emotions: The Guru Knows Themselves** A guru is **hyper-aware** of their emotions. They know exactly what they're feeling and why. There's no sugarcoating or denial. They know what's going on inside them. When they feel anger, they feel it fully, but they don't let it take control. Instead, they observe it. **What's driving it?** Is it a thought? A belief? An unmet need?

They're not afraid of their emotions. They don't suppress them. They simply observe. The first step in emotional mastery is **self-awareness.** Without it, you're just reacting to life, never in control.

1. **Self-Regulation: The Guru Doesn't Let Emotions Hijack Their Life** It's easy to let emotions run wild. **But a guru knows that letting emotions dictate actions leads to chaos.** They understand that the moment they lose control of their emotions, they lose control of their life.

Self-regulation means choosing not to react impulsively. The guru practices **mindfulness**—they pause, they breathe, they step back from the emotional surge. This is the power of **pause.** When you're able to create space between feeling and action, you have the power to decide how you respond. Instead of impulsively reacting, the guru chooses to act intentionally.

Let me give you a real-world example. You're in a meeting, and someone criticizes your work. Your immediate impulse is to get defensive, to lash back, to justify yourself. But if you're following the guru's approach, **you pause.** You breathe. You notice the emotional surge. And then you ask yourself: *What's driving my response?* Is it insecurity? Pride? Fear of being judged?

By doing this, you give yourself time to **respond thoughtfully**. You don't get lost in a cycle of emotional reactivity. You don't add fuel to the fire. Instead, you calmly express your thoughts without being ruled by your emotions.

1. **Empathy: The Guru Understands the Emotions of Others**
   Emotional intelligence isn't just about managing your own emotions. It's also about understanding and empathizing with the emotions of others. A guru can **sense the emotional state of others** and respond with compassion, not judgment. They don't take things personally. They understand that other people's emotions are their own to manage, and they don't get caught up in other people's emotional drama.

When you develop emotional awareness, you begin to see beyond the surface. You understand that behind every emotional reaction is a deeper need, belief, or fear. This doesn't mean you have to agree with someone's emotions, but it does mean you can respond with **understanding**, rather than reacting out of your own emotional triggers.

Practical Exercises for Emotional Mastery

Let's get to work. These exercises will help you develop emotional mastery, so you can **stop being controlled by your emotions** and start responding with clarity and intention.

1. Emotional Check-In

Take a few minutes every day to check in with yourself. Ask yourself: *What am I feeling right now?* Write it down. Identify the emotion. Is it anger? Sadness? Anxiety? Once you identify it, ask yourself why. What triggered this emotion? What's the deeper need or fear behind it?

By doing this daily, you'll build emotional awareness. You'll learn to recognize patterns, and the more you do this, the more easily you'll be able to identify emotions in real-time.

2. The Pause Practice

Next time you feel a strong emotion rising—anger, frustration, fear—**pause**. Literally stop. Take a deep breath. Close your eyes for a moment, and just observe what's happening inside you. What's going on in your mind? What's the physical sensation of the emotion? Where do you feel it in your body?

This practice of **pausing** gives you space between the feeling and the reaction. The more you pause, the less you'll react out of habit.

3. Reframing Emotional Triggers

Take a common emotional trigger in your life—perhaps it's an argument with your partner or a stressful situation at work. The next time it happens, consciously choose to reframe the situation. Instead of reacting with frustration or defensiveness, ask yourself: *What's another way to view this? What's the underlying need or fear driving this emotion?*

By reframing the situation, you break free from automatic emotional responses and regain control over how you react.

The Takeaway: You Are Not Your Emotions

You're not your anger. You're not your fear. **You are the observer of those emotions.** When you can separate yourself from your emotions, you gain control. When you stop being reactive and start being responsive, you tap into the power of emotional mastery.

The modern guru isn't emotionally detached—they're emotionally aware. They don't run from their emotions; they **understand** them. And they don't let them rule their lives. They regulate them. They respond, not react.

Now it's your turn. Practice awareness. Practice self-regulation. Practice empathy. And most importantly, practice **emotional mastery**. Because when you control your emotions, you control your life.

Let's get to work.

Part 3: The Role of Consciousness in Personal Growth

———

Let's get one thing straight: **Self-awareness is the single most powerful tool you'll ever have for personal growth.** If you don't understand yourself—your thoughts, your emotions, your triggers—how can you expect to change anything about your life?

You can talk about goals, you can set intentions, you can have the best plans in the world, but if you're not aware of **what's really going on** inside you, all of that is just wishful thinking. If you want to evolve, if you want to get to the next level—**you have to see yourself clearly.** The guru knows this. That's why awareness is the foundation of everything.

Now, don't mistake awareness for knowledge. Knowledge is intellectual. Awareness is experiential. It's not about knowing facts; it's about **experiencing yourself in the moment.** The more deeply you become aware of your own mind and emotions, the more control you'll have over your life. You won't be at the mercy of your thoughts and feelings anymore. **You'll be the one driving the bus.**

So, let's talk about what that means in practical terms. How do you go from a passive observer of your thoughts and emotions to an active participant in your own growth? How do you cultivate deeper consciousness? This is where the real work begins.

Deep Self-Awareness: The Key to Personal Evolution

To begin with, let's cut through the nonsense. Self-awareness isn't about feeling good about yourself. It's about **seeing yourself clearly**, warts and all. You have to look at the stuff you've been avoiding. The patterns. The habits. The unconscious beliefs that are running the show. And let me tell you right now—this is not always comfortable.

Why? Because when you start to peel back the layers, you realize just how much of your life is being run by autopilot. Your beliefs, your reactions, your choices—they're mostly habitual. And the worst part? You don't even know it.

You might think, "I'm a free thinker. I'm in control of my life." **No, you're not.** Not unless you're actively watching your thoughts, emotions, and behaviors. Without awareness, you're at the mercy of your subconscious programming.

The guru doesn't let this slide. They know that deep awareness of their inner workings is the only way they can evolve. And it's the same for you. Once you realize how much of your behavior is unconscious, you'll see that **personal evolution begins with taking responsibility for what's happening inside you**—all of it.

You don't need to be perfect. You don't need to have it all figured out. But you do need to have **enough awareness to know when you're falling into old patterns.** That's where growth starts.

The Techniques That Build Consciousness

Building consciousness doesn't happen overnight. It's a practice. It's a discipline. It takes effort. But just like lifting weights, the more you practice, the stronger you become.

Here are the two techniques that will turbocharge your awareness:

1. Journaling: The Mirror to Your Soul

One of the simplest, most effective tools to build awareness is **journaling.** And I'm not talking about scribbling down your grocery list or what you did today. **I'm talking about deep, reflective journaling.** This is where you sit down and ask yourself the hard questions.

Here's what you need to do:

- **Write about your emotions.** How are you really feeling? Don't censor yourself. Don't write what you think you're supposed to feel. Write what's actually going on. This isn't a place to put on a happy face. If you're angry, write that down. If you're confused, say it. If you're frustrated, name it. The point isn't to stay stuck in those emotions—it's to become aware of them.

- **Reflect on your triggers.** When did you get upset today? What set you off? Write about it. What do those triggers tell you about your deeper needs or fears? If you find yourself getting angry because someone interrupted you, for example, ask yourself, *What's really going on here? Why do I feel disrespected?* The goal is to start connecting the dots between your emotions and your deeper beliefs.

- **Ask big questions.** What do I want out of life? What's holding me back? What do I believe about myself that's not true? Journaling is the place where you can ask the tough questions. No one is watching. There's no need to impress anyone. Just get it out on paper.

Don't do this once a week and expect magic. **Do this daily.** If you commit to journaling for 10 minutes every day, you'll start to uncover patterns in your thoughts, emotions, and behaviors. Over time, you'll develop a level of awareness that most people never reach in their entire lives. And that's the point.

2. Meditation: The Practice of Being Present with Yourself

Meditation is another technique that will sharpen your awareness. Now, if you've never meditated before, it might sound a little fluffy or even pointless. But don't knock it until you try it. Meditation is simply the practice of **being present with yourself.** It's about learning to sit with your thoughts and emotions without running from them.

Here's how you start:

- **Set a timer for 5-10 minutes.** You don't need to go overboard. Just set aside a small chunk of time to sit quietly.

- **Sit comfortably.** You don't need to sit cross-legged on the floor if that's not comfortable for you. Just find a quiet spot and sit with a straight back.
- **Focus on your breath.** The simplest meditation technique is to pay attention to your breath. In and out. That's it. Every time your mind wanders (and it will), just gently bring it back to your breath.
- **Observe your thoughts.** As you meditate, your thoughts will come and go. Your job isn't to judge them or try to control them. Your job is simply to observe. **Notice what thoughts keep coming up.** Are they about fear? Anger? Doubt? Desire? Without reacting, just **acknowledge** them. This is the first step in building awareness of your inner world.

Meditation teaches you how to stay present with yourself without getting lost in your thoughts. It trains your mind to focus on the **now**, which is where real power lies.

The more you meditate, the more you'll start to notice the thoughts and patterns that run on autopilot. **And when you notice them, you have the power to change them.**

The Guru's Mindset: Why Awareness Leads to Evolution

So why does all this matter? Why does awareness lead to evolution? Because once you see yourself clearly, you can begin to make conscious choices.

Think about it: If you're always operating on autopilot, you're stuck in **default mode.** You react the same way you always have. But once you develop deep self-awareness, you **wake up**. You see the patterns. You see what's working and what's not. And once you see it, you can **change it**. That's evolution.

A guru doesn't change because they "decide" to change. They change because they have the **awareness** to see what needs to shift. They don't just react to life. They **respond** to it. They take conscious action based on their deeper understanding of themselves.

This is where you start to break free from the limiting beliefs and behaviors that have been holding you back. You're no longer at the mercy of your unconscious mind. You become **the creator of your own evolution**.

Action Steps to Strengthen Your Consciousness

1. **Daily Journaling:**
    - Start with 10 minutes a day. Reflect on your emotions, triggers, and beliefs. Write without judgment. Be honest. The more you do this, the more you'll uncover about your unconscious patterns.
2. **Meditation Practice:**
    - Set aside 10 minutes every day to meditate. Focus on your breath. Notice your thoughts. Don't judge them. Just observe. This is how you start to notice your habitual thought patterns and learn to control them.
3. **Reflect on Your Growth:**
    - At the end of each week, take time to look back on your journaling and meditation practice. What have you noticed? What patterns are emerging? What's shifting? Celebrate your awareness, because with it, you're changing.

Final Thoughts: Awareness is Power

You want to grow? You want to evolve? Start by looking at yourself. Start by becoming aware of what's going on inside. You've got to peel back the layers and face the truth, no matter how uncomfortable. **Awareness is the first step toward transformation.** Without it, there's no way forward. But with it, there's nothing you can't change.

Now, take the first step. Get out of your head, out of your excuses, and into your life. **The door to personal evolution is wide open, and it starts with you seeing yourself clearly.**

Part 4: Practical Steps to Increase Awareness

———

Listen up, because this is where you stop just thinking about growth and start actually **doing** the work. Awareness isn't some fluffy, abstract concept to ponder while sipping herbal tea. It's about **practical action**. It's about **tracking**, **noticing**, and **responding**. This is the hard stuff. The real work.

You've heard it before, "be more mindful" or "stay present"—but how? How do you actually build this skill? How do you sharpen your awareness so you're not just drifting through life, reacting to whatever happens to you?

The answer is simple: **Daily practices.** You can't just read about awareness, journal about it, or wish for it. You have to put in the effort every damn day. The guru knows this better than anyone. You've got to develop the habit of noticing your thoughts, your emotions, your reactions, and everything else that's flying under your radar.

This chapter isn't about theories. It's about giving you the tools to **actively cultivate** awareness in your life, **right now**. So, let's dive into the methods that will change everything.

1. The Power of Daily Mindfulness Practices

Start simple. Start small. But **start.**

Mindfulness is the art of noticing what's going on in the present moment. Noticing your thoughts. Noticing your emotions. Noticing the sensations in your body. That's it. Simple, right?

Now, here's the catch: you've been trained your entire life to ignore all of that. To rush, to judge, to multitask, to avoid. So, it's going to take effort to unlearn all that nonsense and **be present**. That's where mindfulness comes in.

Mindfulness Practice: The One-Minute Check-In

This is an easy, yet powerful way to practice mindfulness throughout the day. Every hour, set a timer for just **one minute**. The purpose of this timer isn't to rush you through your day. It's to **interrupt** the autopilot. When that timer goes off, you stop and check in with yourself.

What are you feeling right now? Are you tense? Anxious? Relaxed? Frustrated? Identify it. Don't judge it, just notice it. What's running through your mind? Are you focused on the present moment, or are you ruminating on something from the past or worrying about the future?

Don't rush it. Just take 60 seconds to be fully aware of where you are emotionally, mentally, and physically. No excuses. If you do this even just **once an hour**, you'll build a muscle of awareness that you didn't have before. You'll start catching yourself before you react. You'll begin to see patterns in your behavior, thoughts, and emotions. And that's where real change happens.

2. *The Emotional Trigger Tracker: Understanding Your Reactions*

You want to know the secret to emotional mastery? It's simple: **Track your triggers.**

A trigger is something that sets off a strong emotional reaction. It might be a look from someone, a comment, an event, or even a memory. **Whatever it is, your emotions are reacting before your brain can even process it.** It's automatic.

But here's the problem: most people go through life **unaware** of their triggers. They react without understanding why. They let emotions control them, instead of the other way around.

So, here's what you're going to do: **start tracking your emotional triggers.**

The Emotional Trigger Tracker: Step-by-Step

1. **Get a notebook or an app.** It doesn't matter how you track it, as long as you do it consistently.

2. **Every time you have a strong emotional reaction, write it down.** Doesn't matter if it's anger, sadness, frustration, or even joy. Write it down.

3. **Note what triggered you.** Who or what set you off? What happened in that moment? What was said? What event or circumstance caused your reaction?

4. **Describe how you felt.** Were you angry, sad, anxious? How strong was the emotion? On a scale of 1-10, how intense was the reaction?

5. **Reflect: What's the underlying story?** Here's the kicker. You're not just writing down "I got mad because I was cut off in traffic." No. Dig deeper. Ask yourself: *Why did that trigger me? What's the deeper belief behind it?* Maybe you felt disrespected. Maybe you felt vulnerable or helpless. Start noticing patterns. Over time, you'll see that certain emotional responses come from deeper beliefs you've been holding onto.

This may sound tedious, but trust me—it works. The more you track your emotional responses, the more **you'll begin to see** the underlying stories you're telling yourself. The more you see them, the more control you'll have. You'll start to catch yourself **before** you react.

3. *Thought Awareness: Understanding the Voice in Your Head*

Let's talk about the voice in your head. You know the one. The one that tells you what you should be doing, what you're doing wrong, what others are thinking of you. That voice can be loud and obnoxious—or quiet and insidious. But here's the truth: **you are not your thoughts.**

Most people think their thoughts define them. They think, "I'm a failure," because they think those words in their heads. Or, "I'm not good enough," because their inner voice repeats it over and over again. But guess what? **Your thoughts are not facts.** They're just thoughts. And the more you learn to recognize them as **just thoughts**, the less power they have over you.

So, here's how to start being aware of your thoughts:

The Thought Awareness Exercise:

1. **Pay attention to your thoughts.** Start by noticing what goes on in your mind. What are you telling yourself? Is it negative? Judgmental? Critical? Positive?
2. **Write them down.** When you catch yourself thinking something, write it down. Write down the negative self-talk or the recurring thought patterns. The idea isn't to suppress them. It's to **notice** them.
3. **Ask yourself, "Is this true?"** When a negative thought pops up—like, "I'll never be good enough" or "I'm not capable"—ask yourself, "Is that actually true?" Get curious. Is this thought really accurate, or is it just something your mind is throwing at you to keep you small?
4. **Challenge your thoughts.** If it's not true, rewrite it. If your thought is, "I'm a failure," rewrite it as, "I've had setbacks, but I am capable of learning and improving." Shift the narrative.

By writing down and challenging your thoughts, you take back control from the automatic reactions your mind is feeding you. You start to develop the ability to **consciously choose your thoughts**, rather than just letting them run wild.

4. Grounding Practices: Getting Out of Your Head and Into Your Body

Here's the truth: Your mind is a tool. It's not who you are. And if you let it run the show, it will take you in circles. One way to get back to **awareness**—and to stop being trapped in your thoughts—is through grounding practices. These practices help you get out of your head and back into the **present moment**.

The Grounding Exercise:

1. **Body Awareness.** Sit or stand still. Close your eyes. Start by noticing your body. **How does it feel right now?** Are you tense? Are your shoulders tight? Where are you holding tension?
2. **Deep Breathing.** Take five deep breaths. In through your nose for a count of four, hold for four, and exhale through your mouth for a count of four. Focus only on your breath. In and out. Feel the air entering your body and leaving it.
3. **Five Senses Check-In.** Ground yourself by paying attention to all five senses. What do you see? What do you hear? What do you smell? What do you feel? What do you taste?

These grounding exercises pull you out of your mind's chaos and bring you back to the here and now. It's a simple yet powerful tool to **recenter** yourself when you're overwhelmed, anxious, or lost in thought.

The Takeaway: Building Awareness Requires Consistency

None of these exercises are one-time fixes. You have to practice them every day. That's the key. Consistency is the real secret to unlocking awareness. Whether it's tracking your emotions, challenging your thoughts, or practicing mindfulness, you have to make these tools part of your routine.

Remember: **Awareness is the gateway to personal power.** If you want to take charge of your life, your emotions, and your reactions, you have to start noticing. Right now.

So get out there. Do the work. Be present. Be aware. This is the beginning of your transformation. You can't fake it. You've got to commit. And once you do, the world will change. It all starts with **you seeing yourself clearly**. Now, get to work.

Chapter 4: Compassion and Vulnerability: The Guru's Heart

Part 1: The Power of Compassion

———

Let's be clear about something right from the start: **Compassion isn't a luxury. It's a requirement.** If you want to be a modern guru, a true force in the world, you can't do it without it. Compassion isn't a soft, feel-good idea you pull out when it's convenient. It's the raw, unshakable foundation upon which you build everything else. Without it, you're just another self-absorbed person with some nice ideas. And we don't need more of those.

Now, I know what you're thinking: "I'm compassionate. I'm nice to people." Sure, you may be nice, but that's not compassion. Compassion isn't about being polite, and it sure as hell isn't about being a doormat. Compassion is about **connection**. Real connection. It's about meeting another person where they are, without judgment, and without trying to fix them. Compassion is about seeing the pain, the struggle, the humanity in someone else—and understanding that, at some level, you're no different.

The Guru understands this at the deepest level. They don't look at others and see labels—rich, poor, weak, strong, successful, failed—they see **people**, and they respond with the same heart they would respond to themselves. They don't play games with other people's pain. They don't avoid it, run from it, or try to fix it. They embrace it. They look the discomfort in the face and allow it to exist without any fear or judgment.

If you want to make a real difference in the world, this is where it starts: **Compassion.**

1. The Guru's Approach to Compassion: Non-Judgment, Real Connection

A modern guru doesn't give a damn about your status or your story. They're not concerned with how "successful" you are, how many followers you have, or what your Instagram looks like. **They care about your heart.**

Compassion is about seeing people fully, as they are in that moment—flaws, messiness, and all. When you meet someone with compassion, you don't see them through a filter. You don't look at their behavior and judge them based on their actions. You see the whole person, their circumstances, their struggles, and their humanity.

The key here is **non-judgment**. That doesn't mean you agree with everything someone does, or that you allow toxic behavior in your life. It means you understand **their pain, their fear, their past**. And you meet them with empathy, not condemnation.

A lot of people mistake compassion for sympathy. Sympathy says, "Oh, poor you. I'm sorry you're going through that." **That's not compassion.** Sympathy is pity. Compassion is empathy—**active understanding**. It's not about feeling sorry for someone; it's about feeling with them. It's about standing in the fire with someone and offering the comfort of presence, not platitudes.

Let me tell you about a moment in my life where compassion showed up when I needed it most.

Personal Story: A Lesson in Compassion

A few years ago, I was facing one of the most challenging moments of my life. I had lost everything. **Everything.** I felt like a failure, and it seemed like everyone around me could see it. And in that moment, someone I barely knew came up to me. They didn't say, "Hey, you'll get through this." They didn't give me advice or even try to "fix" my situation.

Instead, they just sat with me. **They just listened.** No judgment. No expectations.

They didn't pity me. They didn't try to change me. They simply let me feel what I was feeling. They allowed me to vent, to be vulnerable, without worrying about how I appeared or what I said. And in that space, I found my own answers. I started to heal—not because someone gave me advice, but because **someone saw me**, in my pain, without judgment. That's real compassion. **That's the guru's heart.**

When you can sit with someone in their pain, in their raw humanity, and not try to fix them, but simply **be with them**, you offer them a space for transformation. You help them reconnect to their own heart.

2. Why Compassion is Key to Personal Transformation

Here's the truth: **you can't transform without compassion**. You can't change your life, grow as a person, or evolve spiritually if you don't practice compassion—**for yourself, and for others**.

Personal transformation requires you to see yourself honestly. It requires you to look at the mess, the mistakes, and the flaws with acceptance, not judgment. It's the same with others. **If you can't see the humanity in others, you'll never see the humanity in yourself.** If you can't meet others with compassion, you'll never meet yourself with compassion.

Most people go through life with a mask on. They hide their flaws, their failures, their pain. They think that if they just push hard enough, act strong enough, or fake it well enough, they'll be good enough. But here's the reality: **that's a lie.** It's the lie that holds you back from your true self.

Compassion is the antidote to that lie. When you can look at your own imperfections, your own struggles, and say, **"This is me. This is where I am. And that's okay,"** you start the process of real transformation. Compassion is what allows you to look in the mirror and love yourself, **not despite your flaws, but because of them.**

When you're compassionate with yourself, you stop resisting what is. You stop fighting against your own imperfections. You stop pretending to be something you're not, and in that authenticity, transformation begins. You can't change what you're not willing to face.

The guru's approach to compassion is **non-judgmental self-acceptance.** They don't hide their flaws. They don't pretend to be perfect. They're **fully human**—and because of that, they can help others heal. When you understand that you're human too—when you drop the need to be perfect—you create the space for true growth.

3. Practical Steps to Cultivate Compassion in Your Life

Now, you might be thinking, "That's all well and good, but how do I actually put this into practice?" You want to be a guru? You want to make a real impact on others and yourself? You want to connect with others from a place of **non-judgment and real empathy**? Then get to work.

Here's what you're going to do:

Step 1: Practice Active Listening

Most people listen to respond. They hear your words, but they're already thinking about what they'll say next. **Stop that.** Start listening to understand. **Listen with your heart.**

When someone talks to you, don't interrupt. Don't think about your response. Don't judge. Just listen. Pay attention to their words, their tone, their emotions. Listen like it's the most important thing in the world.

Step 2: Recognize Your Judgments

We all judge. We do it all the time. But if you want to connect with people, you have to notice your judgments and **let them go**. When you find yourself judging someone—whether it's their behavior, their appearance, their mistakes—**stop**. Take a deep breath. Ask yourself, "What's it like to be them right now?" And, **choose compassion**.

Step 3: Offer Presence, Not Solutions

Most people don't want your solutions. They want your presence. They want someone to stand with them in the storm, not someone to throw them an umbrella. When someone is struggling, just be there. Don't try to fix it. Don't try to solve their problem. Just be present.

Step 4: Practice Self-Compassion

You can't give what you don't have. If you're constantly beating yourself up, you're not going to be able to offer anyone else compassion. Start by being kind to yourself. When you mess up, when you feel down, when you fail—be gentle with yourself. Treat yourself like you'd treat a friend.

The Takeaway: Compassion as a Way of Life

Compassion is not a "nice-to-have" trait. It's **vital** for your own growth and for connecting with others. If you want to change your life, if you want to help others change theirs, it begins with compassion. **Without it, you're just spinning your wheels.**

It's not about being perfect. It's about being **human**—vulnerable, raw, authentic, and present. So, get to work. Practice compassion, **every day**. Not just when it's easy, but especially when it's hard.

Because the world needs more real connection. And it starts with you. **Now.**

Part 2: Vulnerability as Strength

L et's cut the crap. **Vulnerability is not weakness. It's your greatest strength.**

You've been sold a lie. You've been taught that showing any crack in your armor—any hint of emotion or doubt—is some kind of failure. **It's not.** The real failure is pretending to be something you're not, holding up a facade of invulnerability, and missing out on the real connection that can only happen when you let your guard down. If you think "strength" is all about hard edges and never showing your true self, you're living in a prison of your own making. It's time to break out.

To think like a guru, you need to get comfortable with being **real**. You need to own your flaws, your imperfections, your fears. Because **that's where the magic happens.** It's in the rawness, the messiness of your human experience, where connection lives. Vulnerability is the bridge between people. And if you're not willing to cross that bridge, you'll keep running in circles, stuck in shallow interactions and shallow lives.

You're not here to live a safe, surface-level existence. You're here to connect deeply with the world, to leave a legacy, to make an impact. But none of that happens from behind a wall. None of it happens from a place of hiding. **Real strength comes when you open up.** Real strength comes when you are **willing** to show the world who you really are.

Now, let's break it down. Let's talk about how **vulnerability** isn't something to be afraid of. It's your gateway to power. **It's the door to deeper, more authentic connections**, and the key to a more powerful, more meaningful life.

1. Vulnerability Creates Authentic Connection

Here's the truth: **No one trusts someone who pretends to have it all together.** People can spot a fake from a mile away. When you act like you have it all figured out, like you never make mistakes or have bad days, people see that and they pull back. Why? Because it's not real. It's a performance. **And no one connects with a performance.**

People want to connect with the real you, the raw you. The parts of you that aren't perfect. **Vulnerability makes you human.** And when you're human, people trust you. They relate to you. They *see themselves* in you.

You're sitting at a coffee shop, trying to talk to someone, and you feel like you're talking at them, not with them. Why? Because you're hiding behind a wall of "I'm fine" and "Everything's good." You're not showing your true self. You're not letting them in.

But imagine this: you open up. You drop the act. You share your struggle. You admit where you're struggling, where you're not sure what's next. And guess what happens? **They start to trust you. They start to connect with you.** They see your vulnerability and they feel safe enough to share their own. The wall comes down. The conversation becomes real. The connection deepens.

I've seen it over and over again. The more honest I've been about my own struggles, my own imperfections, the deeper the connections I've had with others. **People respect honesty. They respect authenticity.** They don't need you to have it all figured out; they need you to be real.

2. *The Strength of Emotional Transparency*

There's a massive difference between being vulnerable and being emotionally transparent. Vulnerability is about admitting where you're weak, where you're scared, where you're hurt. But emotional transparency takes that a step further. It's about **letting people in**—without hesitation, without shame—into the inner workings of your mind and heart.

Being emotionally transparent isn't easy. It's raw. It's messy. It's terrifying. But it's also where the most powerful shifts in your life will come from.

I'll tell you this right now: **The guru is emotionally transparent.** They don't hide behind a veil of "I'm fine" or "Everything's under control." They stand in their truth, even when it's uncomfortable. They share their highs, their lows, their doubts, their joy. Because **only then can they truly lead.**

Here's something I learned the hard way: **If you hide your emotions, you'll never really connect with others.** You'll keep people at arm's length, and you'll wonder why you feel so disconnected. Why your relationships feel shallow. Why you're always "busy," but never truly engaged.

Emotional transparency isn't about oversharing or dumping your emotional baggage on others. It's about **being honest and clear** about where you are emotionally, without expecting someone to fix you. It's about saying, "This is what I'm feeling. This is what I'm thinking. This is where I am right now." It's the ultimate act of courage.

3. *The Modern Guru's Approach to Vulnerability: Ownership, Not Victimhood*

Here's where most people screw it up. They think that vulnerability means **victimhood.** They think that showing their emotions means "I'm weak" or "I'm out of control." That's not vulnerability. That's playing the victim.

Real vulnerability, the kind that transforms lives, is about **ownership**. It's about standing up and saying, "This is who I am. This is where I am. And I'm going to take responsibility for my emotions, my actions, and my growth."

The modern guru doesn't sit around wallowing in their emotions. They don't say, "Woe is me. Life is hard. I can't handle it." No. The guru says, "This is what I'm going through, and I'm choosing to grow through it. I'm not a victim. I'm an agent of change. I'm taking responsibility for my story."

When you own your vulnerability, you transform it from something that holds you back into something that empowers you. You **take control**. You stop letting your emotions control you. You stop letting your fears dictate your actions. And you move forward with courage, with authenticity, and with strength.

4. Practical Steps to Embrace Vulnerability as Strength

If you want to step into your full potential and think like a guru, you need to **practice vulnerability**. Not in some passive way, but actively, deliberately. **Here's how to get started:**

Step 1: Acknowledge Your Fear

Let's be real: You're scared. You're scared of what people will think if they see your true self. You're scared of being judged, rejected, or ridiculed. But that fear? It's just a barrier you've built in your mind. Acknowledge it, and move through it.

Write down what you're afraid of. Be specific. Then ask yourself, "Is this fear based in reality, or is it just something I've imagined?" Fear has no power unless you give it power. **So stop giving it power.**

Step 2: Practice Radical Honesty

Start small. The next time someone asks you how you're doing, don't say "fine" if you're not. Be honest. If you're struggling, say it. If you're feeling great, say it. **Don't hide.** Radical honesty is the first step to becoming emotionally transparent.

Step 3: Share Your Story

Vulnerability isn't just about admitting when you're down; it's about sharing your truth in all its forms. Share your wins, your losses, your lessons. **Share it with the people who matter**—your friends, your family, your coworkers, your followers. **Let them see the real you.** It might be scary at first, but you'll start to realize that the more you share, the more people connect with you.

Step 4: Let Go of Perfection

You are not perfect, and that's okay. **Perfection is a myth.** Stop pretending to be something you're not. Stop hiding behind the mask of "having it all together." **Be human.** Be messy. Be flawed. The world will respect you more for it.

The Takeaway: Vulnerability is Power

Here's the bottom line: **Vulnerability is not weakness. It's your strength.** When you embrace it, when you let down your walls, you create the space for **real connection**, for **authentic relationships**, and for **true personal growth**. You become unstoppable.

So, if you want to step into your power as a modern guru, get comfortable with being vulnerable. Show the world who you are. Let your rawness, your authenticity, and your humanity shine through. **It's time to stop hiding.**

You are **more powerful than you realize**, and the moment you embrace vulnerability, you'll unlock a level of strength you never knew existed.

Now, go show up—fully, unapologetically, and with your heart wide open.

Part 3: The Guru's View on Suffering

Let's get one thing straight: **Suffering is not something to run from.** It's not something to avoid. It's not a sign that you're doing it wrong or that life has handed you a bad hand. **Suffering is part of the game.** Period.

You're not here to have a smooth ride. You're here to experience life—every inch of it, even the parts that sting. The sooner you accept this, the sooner you'll stop fighting it and start learning from it. And make no mistake, there's **wisdom in suffering**. There's power in pain. If you're not embracing your suffering, you're missing the point of this whole damn thing.

You want to think like a modern guru? Then stop pretending your suffering isn't real. Stop acting like you've got it all figured out, like you're immune to the hard stuff. **You're not.** And that's okay.

The guru doesn't shrink from suffering. **The guru welcomes it**. Not because they're masochistic, not because they think pain is inherently good, but because they understand that suffering is a teacher—a teacher with lessons that no textbook can provide. It's not about the pain; it's about what you do with it. Do you let it crush you, or do you let it shape you?

You're going to suffer. That's a guarantee. The question is: **What are you going to do with it?**

1. Suffering as a Path to Wisdom

We live in a world that wants to fix everything. You get hurt, you take a pill. You're in pain, you get therapy. You're struggling emotionally, you seek comfort in distractions. The world tells you that suffering is something to eliminate, avoid, or numb. But here's the truth you need to hear:

Suffering is the vehicle of wisdom.

If you want to grow—truly grow—you have to be willing to sit with your pain. Because here's the dirty secret: **Pain doesn't just go away on its own.** It comes up to be faced, to be dealt with. If you ignore it, shove it down, or run from it, you're just going to keep seeing it again and again in different forms.

The modern guru understands this. The guru knows that every painful experience, every moment of suffering, is an opportunity to learn something new about themselves. **That's the key to growth.**

Suffering teaches you **patience**. It teaches you **resilience**. It teaches you **compassion**, because when you've been through hell, you develop an empathy that can't be taught in any book.

You want wisdom? You want deep understanding? Then you need to embrace the lessons that suffering brings. The next time you face hardship, instead of asking "Why me?" ask **"What can I learn from this?"** Because there's always something to learn.

2. *The Illusion of Escaping Pain*

Here's the thing you need to understand: **You can't escape suffering.** It's not something you get to bypass. It's woven into the fabric of existence, like a thread you can't cut out. And pretending it's not there, ignoring it, or running away from it only makes it worse.

The guru doesn't avoid suffering. They don't look for ways to push through it faster, to cover it up with distractions or quick fixes. **They lean into it.** They feel it. They don't resist it. They know that fighting against pain is like fighting the tide—it only exhausts you.

You think avoiding pain makes you stronger? No. It makes you weaker. Because when you run from pain, you run from the opportunity to grow. The more you deny it, the more it has power over you.

Stop trying to escape it. **Sit with it.** Feel it fully. And when you do, you'll start to see that it's not nearly as powerful as you thought it was. Pain is temporary. But the wisdom it brings? **That's forever.**

3. Techniques for Embracing Pain as a Path to Wisdom

So how do you turn suffering into wisdom? How do you take the pain you're experiencing right now and use it to evolve into a stronger, more resilient person? Let's talk about some techniques that will help you face pain, not just endure it, but use it to propel you forward.

Step 1: Acknowledge It

The first step is always **acknowledgment**. You can't work with pain if you're in denial about it. So stop pretending. If you're hurting, admit it. If you're struggling, say it. Call it what it is. **The truth is the first step to transformation.**

You might be scared of what's coming up, or ashamed that you're in pain. **Get over it.** Everyone suffers. Everyone. The only difference is how you handle it.

Start journaling about what you're feeling. **Get specific.** Name your pain, your fears, your struggles. Write them down, and then ask yourself, "What is this trying to teach me?" Write your thoughts out. You might be surprised at what comes up. **Acknowledge your suffering and allow it to exist without judgment.**

Step 2: Shift Your Perspective

Once you've acknowledged the pain, the next step is to **shift your perspective.** Instead of seeing suffering as something to avoid, see it as a teacher. Ask yourself, "What wisdom can I gain from this?"

You're facing a setback? Maybe it's a broken relationship, a financial problem, or a health issue. **Instead of feeling like the universe is against you**, shift your thinking. Ask, "What is this situation showing me about myself?"

Suffering strips away the excess, leaving you with the raw truth. When you're in pain, there's no hiding behind your ego, your pride, or your distractions. **The truth will come to the surface.**

It's easy to want to fix things, to want to escape the pain. But sometimes, **pain is the answer**. It's showing you where you need to grow, what you need to learn, or where you've been avoiding the truth.

Step 3: Allow Yourself to Feel Fully

So often, we try to suppress our emotions. We think that if we ignore them, they'll go away. They don't. They only fester. **If you want to use pain as a path to wisdom, you need to feel it.**

This isn't about wallowing in misery or staying stuck in sadness. This is about **giving yourself permission to feel what you're feeling** without shame or judgment. When you feel pain, let it wash over you. Sit with it. Honor it. Don't try to rush through it.

You might feel anger, grief, frustration. Good. Feel it all. When you do, you'll notice something incredible: the more you allow yourself to feel, the more you start to detach from the pain. You don't become the pain. You just experience it, and then let it pass.

Step 4: Use the Pain to Fuel Action

Here's where the guru mindset kicks in. **You don't wallow in suffering.** You use it to fuel action. When you're in pain, it's a sign that something in your life needs to change. Something needs to shift.

Ask yourself: "What can I do differently next time? How can I grow from this experience?" Use the insights you've gained from feeling the pain to make a plan. The guru doesn't sit around and complain. They take action.

Whether that means setting new boundaries, changing your mindset, or seeking out support, take concrete steps to transform your suffering into **action.**

The Takeaway: Suffering is Your Ally

Here's the bottom line: **Suffering is your ally**, not your enemy. It's not something to be feared or avoided. It's the path to deeper wisdom, the fuel for your personal evolution. If you want to grow, if you want to live a life that matters, you have to embrace your suffering.

The modern guru doesn't run from pain. They face it. They learn from it. They grow from it. So the next time you're struggling, the next time you're in pain, remember: this is your opportunity to become who you're meant to be. This is your chance to learn the lessons that will propel you forward.

So stop fighting the pain. Embrace it. Lean into it. **And let it show you what you're made of.**

Part 4: Practicing Compassion and Vulnerability

———

Listen up. **You can't skip this step.** Compassion and vulnerability are not optional if you want to truly evolve. If you want to become a modern guru, you have to *live* these qualities every single day. It's not about reading about them or nodding your head in agreement when you hear some guru on a podcast talk about them. It's about showing up, heart open, and practicing them when it counts. In real life. When it's hard.

Let's talk about what that looks like, step by step. This isn't some abstract idea or feel-good concept. We're talking about raw, real, gritty action. Compassion isn't something you just "feel"; it's something you *do*. Vulnerability isn't something you simply accept about yourself; it's something you *practice*.

You want to be a guru? Then **stop hiding.** Stop pretending. Stop shielding yourself with layers of armor. It's time to show up fully, heart exposed, and be present with others—and with yourself. Let's break it down.

1. Opening the Heart: The Practice of Compassion

You can't fake compassion. It's not a buzzword. It's a muscle that needs to be built. And like any muscle, if you don't work it out, it gets weak. But when you practice compassion, you start seeing the world differently. You start seeing people differently.

Compassion means that when you look at someone—whether it's a friend, a stranger, or even an enemy—you see them as human. You see their pain, their struggles, their stories. And instead of turning away or judging, you feel for them. **You understand.** You don't need to have all the answers, but you stand in their shoes for a moment.

But let's get one thing straight: **Compassion is not about saving people.** You're not a martyr. You're not a savior. You're a human being who recognizes the shared experience of suffering, and you offer your presence. Your understanding. Your willingness to be there, without judgment, and without needing anything in return.

Compassion is the opposite of indifference. You know how it feels when someone truly sees you, truly listens to you, and truly cares. You also know how it feels when someone ignores you, judges you, or acts like you don't matter. The difference is night and day. **Compassion is the bridge that connects us all.**

Now, I know you've probably had moments where you wanted to shut down, to close off, to say, "I'm done." You've been hurt. You've been disappointed. And the natural instinct is to harden yourself. But that's **weakness**, not strength.

Compassion takes strength. It takes courage. **It takes you stepping outside of yourself** and truly connecting with another human being, even when you're tired, even when it's inconvenient, even when they've hurt you. Compassion doesn't always feel comfortable, but it's the key to deepening relationships, building trust, and connecting with others in a way that creates lasting impact.

2. *Practicing Vulnerability: The Courage to Be Real*

Vulnerability is not a weakness. In fact, **it's your greatest strength.** Don't buy into the lie that being strong means shutting down your emotions, hiding your true self, or pretending everything is okay when it's not. **Vulnerability is what makes you human.** It's what makes you authentic. And **authenticity is magnetic.**

When you're vulnerable, you're allowing yourself to be seen, flaws and all. You're opening up to others and letting them know, "Hey, I don't have all the answers. I don't have it all together. But I'm here. I'm real. And I'm willing to show up."

And guess what? **People respond to that.** Because when you let your guard down, others feel safe to do the same. You create an environment where true connection can happen—where people can be themselves, drop their facades, and feel accepted for who they are, not who they think they need to be.

Let me tell you something: **Vulnerability is the antidote to isolation.** It's the remedy for loneliness. It's the key to intimacy, whether in a friendship, a relationship, or a team. If you want to connect with others, if you want to lead others, **you have to be willing to go first.**

The more you open up, the more you'll realize that everyone else is just as scared as you are. Everyone else is just as uncertain. Everyone else is wondering if they're enough. When you show up vulnerably, you give others permission to do the same.

3. Exercises to Open Your Heart and Practice Empathy

Now, let's get to work. No more theory. **This is the stuff that separates the talkers from the doers.**

Exercise 1: Empathy in Action

Here's the deal: you're going to practice empathy with someone today. It could be a family member, a friend, a colleague, or even a stranger. The goal is simple: **Be present.** Listen deeply. Let go of judgment, let go of advice, and let go of trying to fix the situation. Just listen. **Without interruption.**

When you listen, listen as if you've never heard their story before. Listen without trying to form a response in your head. Your job is to absorb, not to solve. It's about understanding, not fixing.

Here's how to do it:

1. Find someone who's open to talking.
2. Listen to them as if their words are the most important thing in the world. Don't think about what you'll say next.

3. When they're done, ask, "How can I support you?" or "How do you feel about this situation?"
4. If they need space, give it. If they need your advice, offer it gently—but don't assume they want it.
5. Reflect back what you heard them say. Use phrases like, "It sounds like you're feeling..." or "I hear you saying..."

Repeat this every day. **This is compassion in action.**

Exercise 2: Vulnerability Journaling Prompt

Now it's time to do some deep self-reflection. **Vulnerability isn't just about being open with others.** It starts with being open with yourself. Grab a journal. Find a quiet space. And get honest with yourself about where you're hiding.

Write the following:

- **What am I afraid to share about myself?** What do I keep hidden from others because I fear judgment?
- **Where in my life am I pretending to be something I'm not?** How am I putting up walls to protect myself from being hurt or rejected?
- **When was the last time I was truly vulnerable with someone?** What did that experience teach me? How did it feel to open up?
- **Who in my life do I need to show up for, authentically and vulnerably?** What would it look like if I took the first step?

After you've written, sit with it. **Let the vulnerability sink in.** No more distractions. No more excuses. This is the heart of spiritual growth.

4. Bringing It All Together: Compassion and Vulnerability as Daily Practices

You want to think like a guru? Then you need to make compassion and vulnerability a non-negotiable part of your life. This isn't about being perfect. This is about being real.

- **Compassion** is about connecting with others without judgment, offering your presence and empathy, and showing up for people when they need you most.
- **Vulnerability** is about showing up for yourself first, being real about who you are, and having the courage to let others see the true, unguarded version of you.

Start small. Every day, make it a practice to open your heart to one person. Every day, take a step towards being more vulnerable. Share something about yourself you've been hiding. **No more hiding.** No more walls.

If you do this—if you practice compassion and vulnerability—you'll be unstoppable. **You'll be living like a guru.** And trust me, that's the kind of power that changes the world.

Chapter 5: Living with Purpose: The Guru's Vision for Life

Part 1: Discovering Your Purpose

Listen closely. **If you think your purpose is just about climbing the corporate ladder, chasing accolades, or impressing others with your achievements, you're dead wrong.** Purpose isn't about external validation. It's not about the title, the paycheck, or the shiny trophy on your shelf. If that's all you're after, you're missing the point of your life. And let me tell you something—you don't get to skate by on empty goals for long. That hollow pursuit will eat you alive.

Purpose comes from within. It's the fire in your gut that drives you. It's the thing that keeps you up at night with excitement, but also the thing that makes you restless when you're not aligned with it. This isn't something you can buy, and it's not something you'll find on a weekend retreat with a "guru" handing you a blueprint for success. **Your purpose is a process of discovery, not a destination.**

I know what you're thinking: "How the hell do I figure out what my purpose really is?" I'm going to tell you exactly how to uncover it. But before we get into the nuts and bolts of it, you need to understand this: **Purpose isn't something you discover when everything's perfect.** It's not about waiting until you're successful, happy, or have all the answers. Purpose emerges when you show up—flawed, messy, uncertain, and fully human. And the only way to find it is by starting where you are. Right now.

Let's get to it.

1. Forget About What Society Says

First off, forget the stories society told you about what success looks like. There are plenty of voices out there telling you to hustle harder, work longer, and measure your worth by the number of zeros in your bank account or the status of your job title. You've heard it all before: "Success is a bigger house, a fatter paycheck, a bigger car, a bigger ego." But **none of that tells you who you really are.** And none of it will fill the hole that's in your chest when you're lying awake at night wondering, "What's the point of all this?"

Do yourself a favor: **stop measuring your worth by external metrics.** Those are illusions, distractions. They may seem like the goal, but they're just the packaging. The real prize lies somewhere deeper.

The guru's view on purpose is simple: **Your purpose has nothing to do with what the world expects from you.** Your purpose is not defined by your job title, your salary, or the way others see you. It's about something far more fundamental.

2. *Looking Inside: Purpose is a Personal Discovery*

Now that you've kicked the external noise to the curb, it's time to look within. **Purpose isn't something you find by searching the world around you.** It's something that's already there, buried under all your distractions, fears, and misconceptions about who you think you should be.

Here's the kicker: **You've known your purpose all along.** But somewhere along the way, you got lost in what you were supposed to do, rather than what you were born to do.

Let me break it down with a story from my own life. When I first started out, I was obsessed with building an image. I was trying to fit into what I thought success looked like: climbing the ladder, gaining recognition, becoming "somebody." But every time I reached a goal, it felt like there was something missing. It was as if I was playing someone else's game, running someone else's race. It wasn't until I stopped—**stopped chasing the validation of others, stopped following the herd, stopped running for the wrong reasons**—that I started to hear that quiet voice inside me. It was telling me what I really wanted to do, who I really wanted to be, and what I truly wanted to contribute.

Your purpose isn't found in external recognition, and it's not even something you find after reading ten self-help books. Your purpose is found in **your inner truth.** And it's been there all along, waiting for you to stop pretending it doesn't matter.

You must sit with yourself. If you want to discover your purpose, you need to tune in to your intuition. Stop listening to the world for a moment, and listen to what feels right to *you*. Purpose often emerges when you start stripping away the distractions and ask yourself one crucial question:

What do I want to give the world that no one else can give?

That's where the magic happens. **Purpose is not about receiving. It's about giving.** It's about identifying your unique gifts and figuring out how to offer them to others.

3. *What's Your Unique Gift?*

Let's get specific. **Your gift is what comes easily to you,** what you're passionate about, and what others see in you without you even having to try. It's that thing that, when you're doing it, time seems to stop.

So here's a powerful exercise for you: **Write down your talents, your passions, and the things that excite you.** Don't think about how marketable they are or how other people will respond. Just list everything that makes you feel alive, anything that gives you energy, anything you can't wait to share.

Now, once you have that list, ask yourself: **What is the one thing that would make me feel fulfilled if I could do it every day for the rest of my life?**

This is where you stop listening to everyone else and start listening to *you*. What's your contribution? It's not something that's going to show up in a five-year plan. It's a discovery. And you'll find it by being real with yourself.

4. *The Guru's Approach: Purpose Through Service*

Now, let's talk about the big picture. **Purpose, in the eyes of a guru, is never just about you.** It's about what you give to the world. Your gifts are meant to be shared. They're not yours to hoard.

The world needs your purpose. **It's your responsibility** to bring your gifts to the world. That's the secret of the guru's approach to purpose: **Living for something greater than yourself.** It's about service, not self-centered gain.

I don't care if you're the CEO of a Fortune 500 company or a stay-at-home parent. **Purpose is about being of service,** whether that's through a business, a relationship, a creative pursuit, or a simple act of kindness. What matters is how you use your unique talents to impact the lives of others.

The guru doesn't worry about *what* they're doing—they're focused on *why* they're doing it. And the "why" is always about others. Whether you're building a business or teaching a child, the real question is: How is this helping the world? How is this serving something bigger than me?

5. Embrace the Journey, Not the Destination

Here's the truth: **Purpose is not a one-time discovery.** It's a process. You don't just "find" your purpose and then coast the rest of your life. Purpose is something you have to nurture, refine, and align with as you grow. It evolves with you.

Don't be in a rush to "figure it out." The more you try to force the process, the more you'll get in your own way. **Purpose reveals itself when you stop searching for it and simply start living it.** It's about committing to your truth, showing up for yourself and others, and being willing to adapt as you go.

The guru's path is never linear. It's full of twists, turns, and unexpected lessons. But if you keep moving forward, if you remain open to the process, your purpose will become clearer over time. **And the more you live it, the more fulfilling it becomes.**

Take Action:

1. **Sit down and reflect on what excites you.** Write down your talents, passions, and the things that make you feel alive. What are you naturally good at? What do you love to do, and what can't you stop thinking about?
2. **Ask yourself: How can I serve the world with these gifts?** How can I make a difference, big or small, with what I have? This is your purpose in action.
3. **Take one small step toward living your purpose today.** It doesn't have to be perfect or grand, but do something that moves you closer to serving others with your unique gifts.

And remember—purpose is a journey, not a destination. Keep showing up, keep listening to your heart, and keep giving your gifts to the world. That's the true path of the modern guru.

Part 2: Aligning with Your Values

———

Listen up—if you're not living according to your values, then you're living a lie. **You can't claim to have purpose if you don't even know what's guiding your actions.** Values are the foundation of everything. They're the invisible compass that should steer your ship. If you're unclear on your values, you're not steering anything. You're drifting, getting tossed around by the wind, the waves, the opinions of others, and every external distraction.

But here's the deal: **Purpose is only meaningful when it's anchored in what you truly value.** And those values? They come from deep inside. They aren't something you pick up from a self-help book or from following someone else's advice. They're an inherent part of who you are. You don't need to "find" them. **You need to remember them** and then put them into action, consistently. **Living in alignment with your values is non-negotiable**—if you don't, you're setting yourself up for misery.

So let's break this down. I'm not here to sugarcoat it. You need to get serious about this if you want to live with purpose. You need to act in a way that reflects your core values. **If your actions don't reflect what you truly believe in, you're nothing but a hypocrite.** And that'll eat you from the inside out.

1. Know Your Core Values: No Excuses

You can't align with values you haven't defined. If you think your values are just a list of buzzwords that sound good in a conversation, you're dead wrong. Your core values are *the non-negotiables* of your life—the things that shape how you show up in the world. They should be the foundation for every decision you make, whether it's in your personal relationships, your work, or how you carry yourself in the world.

You may be thinking, "I don't even know what my values are. How do I find them?" I'll tell you how. You **sit down and reflect**. Write it out. You've got to take the time to identify what really matters to you—not what the world tells you should matter, but what *you* value at your core.

Here's how to do it:

- **Step 1: List your top 5 values.** What are the things that *must* be true for you to feel fulfilled? Integrity? Family? Freedom? Growth? Courage? Get specific. Write them down.
- **Step 2: Rank them in order of importance.** Which one is #1, and which one is #5? There's no room for ambiguity here. If it's truly important, it deserves the top spot.
- **Step 3: Examine your actions.** Are your daily decisions in line with your values? If your top value is family, but you spend 80% of your time at the office, you need to reconsider your priorities. **Your actions need to match your values.**

You think you know your values, but the real test is in the follow-through. **If your actions aren't reflecting your values, then you're living in conflict.** The pain of living out of alignment with your core beliefs is unbearable—it'll eat away at you. **You have to be ruthless with yourself.** No more excuses.

2. Integrity: The Backbone of Purpose

Let's talk about integrity—because if you're not walking the walk, you're not going to get very far on your purpose-driven journey. Integrity is about being true to your word, your actions, and your core values. **It's about being consistent with who you are—inside and out.**

When you operate with integrity, your life feels unified. You don't have to put on a mask depending on who you're around. You don't have to second-guess whether you're being authentic or not. When you're living with integrity, everything aligns. But when you're out of integrity, you'll feel it—there's a disconnect. You'll feel the weight of your lies, your inconsistencies, and the compromises you make to please others or get ahead.

Think about it this way: If your core value is honesty, but you consistently lie or withhold the truth, what's going to happen? You'll be living in constant cognitive dissonance. **You'll feel like a fraud.** And that's one of the most miserable experiences a person can have. You'll start questioning who you are, what you stand for, and why you're even doing what you're doing.

The guru is a man or woman of integrity. Their actions reflect their values. There's no pretending. They don't cut corners or compromise on what they know to be true. And this is something you need to embody. If you claim to value health but constantly neglect your body, you're lying to yourself. If you claim to value family but you're never home for dinner, you're out of integrity. **You're lying to the world and to yourself.**

3. Authenticity: The Key to True Alignment

Now, let's talk about authenticity. Integrity is a necessary foundation, but authenticity is the layer that builds upon it. **Authenticity is living as the true version of yourself.** Not the version you think people want you to be. Not the version that's expected of you. **The authentic version of you—the one that shows up when no one is watching.**

This is where a lot of people get lost. They put on masks for different situations, and over time, those masks start to feel like the real them. But here's the thing: **You can't align your life with your purpose if you're constantly pretending to be someone you're not.** You have to step into your own skin, accept who you are, and live in that space.

I've been there. When I first started my journey, I was all about fitting into what I thought was the "right" mold. I thought I had to be a certain way, talk a certain way, do certain things to succeed. But it wasn't until I stopped pretending—until I started showing up **fully myself**, flaws and all—that I felt the power of living with purpose.

This doesn't mean you're perfect. It means you're **real. Authenticity requires courage.** It requires the courage to show up as you are, even if it doesn't fit into someone else's idea of success. And **that's what will set you free.**

4. Aligning Your Actions with Your Values

If you truly want to live with purpose, your actions must align with your values and integrity. Every day, you need to ask yourself: **Are the choices I'm making today aligned with my core values?** If the answer is no, you've got work to do. Simple as that.

Here's a simple exercise to keep you on track:

- **At the end of each day, reflect.** Look back at your actions. Did you show up as your authentic self? Did you make decisions that reflected your values? If not, ask yourself: *Why not? What was holding me back?*
- **Tomorrow, do it differently.** You don't have to be perfect. But the goal is to get closer every day to living in full alignment with your values. Consistency is what builds integrity.

This isn't about becoming some idealized version of yourself. It's about becoming more *authentically* you every single day. **Align your actions with your values, and you will be unstoppable.**

5. The Guru's Call: Be Your Own Master

The guru doesn't wait for external validation. The guru doesn't seek approval. The guru aligns with his or her inner truth and lets that truth dictate the course of life. The guru is **authentic**, grounded in values that can never be shaken by the whims of others. **The guru doesn't follow the crowd—they lead from within.**

And here's the final piece of advice: **Be the guru in your own life.** Step into your truth. Align your actions with your core values. Live with integrity. Don't make excuses. **No one else is going to do it for you.** It's on you to take ownership and do the work.

You want to live with purpose? Then stop lying to yourself. Start aligning your life with your values, and watch everything else fall into place. It's that simple.

Part 3: The Guru's Life Mission

———

Alright, listen up. If you think your purpose is just about making a paycheck, getting the car, the house, the Instagram followers, and living in a nice neighborhood, then you're missing the point. **The real purpose of life isn't about you.** It's not about your personal gain or your comfort zone. Your purpose is about service. **It's about how you can contribute to the world, to humanity, and to the greater good.**

The guru knows this instinctively. The guru's life is not self-serving—it's selfless. **The guru is a servant.** And this isn't some martyr complex. No. It's about understanding that the true fulfillment in life comes when you step out of your ego and into the service of others. **This is the guru's mission**—and it should be yours, too.

But here's where you need to get real with yourself: **If you're not serving others, you're just existing.** And existence? That's not a purpose. That's a waste of time.

1. The Spiritual Dimension of Purpose

If you're serious about living with purpose, then you need to understand that **purpose isn't just a personal mission; it's a spiritual one.** You're here for a reason. Whether you believe in a higher power or the universe, there's something bigger than you at play. And **your purpose is tied into that larger cosmic plan.** The guru knows this. They don't just operate out of their own will—they align with the flow of life, of spirit, and of consciousness.

The spiritual dimension of purpose isn't some abstract concept or a fluffy idea that you see on Instagram motivational quotes. **It's the truth.** It's the foundation of all true purpose. Think of it this way: if you were just born to acquire things and satisfy your immediate desires, that would be a shallow life. **Purpose is something that elevates you, that pushes you beyond your personal limitations and invites you to serve.**

If you're unclear about what that means, start by asking yourself: **What is my contribution? Who needs me?** And when you ask this, don't just think about your career or your social circle. Think about humanity at large. What can you do to uplift the collective? **You want to find real purpose?** You find a way to serve others with everything you've got. Because when you start giving, you receive something much deeper than any material possession can ever give you: **fulfillment.**

2. *The Guru's Role in Serving Humanity*

The guru knows their life is dedicated to serving others. They understand the difference between being a taker and being a giver. **They don't serve to get recognition, approval, or accolades.** They serve because that's what their soul is called to do. And here's the kicker: **when you serve, you align yourself with something much greater than yourself.** You align yourself with the universe's purpose. **When you give, you become part of a much bigger story.**

But let's get clear about this—serving humanity isn't about being a doormat or letting others walk all over you. **Service is a conscious, deliberate act.** It's about choosing to use your unique skills, talents, and experiences to make the world a better place. **It's about showing up and giving your best self, every single day.**

For the guru, every action—whether small or large—is an offering. Every word spoken is an opportunity to lift someone else up. **You want to find your purpose?** Serve others. Start with the people closest to you—your family, your friends, your colleagues—but never stop there. Expand your reach. Find ways to impact the world. It doesn't matter if you're a teacher, an artist, a business owner, or a janitor. Your life is an offering. **And it's your job to make that offering count.**

Here's something to think about: **The more you give, the more you grow.** The guru understands this. They don't serve to exhaust themselves. They serve to evolve. Every act of service is a chance to deepen their understanding of themselves, their purpose, and their connection to the world around them.

The guru's life is not just about 'doing' for others, but about *becoming* someone who embodies love, compassion, and wisdom.

3. How Service and Contribution Can Become a Central Part of Your Purpose

I know what you're thinking. "I've got bills to pay, kids to feed, a job to do. Where am I supposed to fit in this whole service thing?"

Listen, you can't ignore your obligations, but **you can integrate service into everything you do.** Start small. Start with what's right in front of you. Whether it's helping a co-worker, offering a kind word to someone who's struggling, or volunteering in your community, **service can and should be built into your daily life.**

The key here is **mindset.** You don't have to make a grand gesture to have purpose. It's not about becoming Mother Teresa. It's about shifting your focus. Instead of focusing on what you can get out of every situation, shift to: **What can I give here?** That's the question that will radically transform your sense of purpose.

Start by doing a **self-audit.** Look at your current life. **Are you focused mostly on your own needs, your own ambitions?** Or are you making space for others? **How much of your life is centered around contributing to others' well-being?**

If the answer is "not enough," then get to work. And here's a **practical action plan** to help you integrate service into your life:

1. **Identify Your Gifts**: What are you good at? What unique skills do you bring to the table? The guru doesn't just serve from a place of obligation—they serve from their strengths, their passions. Get clear on what you're good at and start thinking about how you can use those skills to help others.
2. **Start Small**: Don't wait for some big opportunity to fall into your lap. **Begin today with the people around you**—family, friends, coworkers, strangers. Every interaction is an opportunity to serve.

Look for the small ways you can make someone's day easier or brighter.

3. **Ask the Question**: In every situation you find yourself in, ask: **How can I serve here?** When you walk into a room, when you get into a conversation, when you make a decision—ask that question. **Your answers will reveal where you're being called to contribute.**

4. **Serve Beyond Comfort**: Real service often involves discomfort. It means putting someone else's needs ahead of your own. It might require time, energy, or sacrifice. **But if you're serious about living a purpose-driven life, you'll have to embrace discomfort.**

5. **Reflect and Adjust**: At the end of each week, take a moment to reflect. **Did I live with a spirit of service?** What could I have done better? How can I show up more fully for others in the coming week?

4. The Guru's Legacy: The Impact of a Life Dedicated to Service

A life dedicated to service isn't just about what you do today. **It's about the legacy you leave behind.** The guru knows that their work is bigger than them. The impact they have ripples outward. **When you dedicate your life to serving others, you create an energy that spreads far beyond your immediate circle.**

You may never know the full extent of your impact. **But when you serve from the heart, when you give without expectation, you create a legacy of love, compassion, and wisdom.** The guru lives for that. The guru knows that their life isn't just about personal success—it's about creating a positive, lasting impact on the world.

5. Your Call to Action

Here's the final message: **Get out of your head and into your heart.** Stop thinking that purpose is about your personal ambitions and goals. Your true purpose is about **how you can serve the greater good.**

The guru's life mission is clear: to serve, to give, to elevate others. **You have that same mission.** But it's up to you to step into it. **Stop waiting for permission. Live with purpose.** Start serving today. That's where real fulfillment lies. And once you start, you won't just change the world—you'll change yourself.

Get out there and serve. The world needs you. Your purpose awaits.

Part 4: Creating a Life Vision

Let's get straight to it. You're not here to float through life like a leaf on the wind, hoping for the best. **You're here to make an impact, to create something bigger than yourself.** If you're not living with intention, then what are you doing? You're just wasting time. No one achieves greatness without a clear, unwavering vision of who they want to become, and what they want to contribute to the world.

The **guru** lives by a powerful and clear vision. They don't drift aimlessly. They don't let life happen to them. **They direct their energy and actions toward a vision of life that's meaningful and purposeful.** This vision is their guiding light. It doesn't matter what gets thrown their way. The guru knows who they are and where they're going. Do you?

If you want to lead a life with purpose, you need to create your own vision. And not just any vision. **A life vision that's aligned with your core values, your strengths, and your deepest truths.** This is the path to living a fulfilling and impactful life. Not some half-hearted, mediocre existence. **No, you're here to make a difference.**

Let's break it down, step by step.

1. The Importance of Creating a Vision

A vision is more than just a goal or a dream. **It's the big picture.** It's the roadmap that keeps you focused when things get tough. If you don't have a clear vision, then you're just wandering around, hoping to land somewhere meaningful. But hope alone won't get you there. **You need clarity.** You need a vision that pulls you forward, especially on the days when you're ready to give up.

The guru lives with a crystal-clear sense of purpose. They see themselves in the context of something greater. They know that **their purpose is to serve**

others, to make an impact, and to contribute to the world. Their vision centers around this idea, and everything they do is in alignment with it.

You need that clarity. **You need to know exactly what you're here to do.** And if you don't know yet, that's fine. **But you better start figuring it out—fast.**

2. Creating a Vision Aligned with Your Purpose

If you haven't figured out your purpose yet, now's the time to get serious about it. **Your purpose is the foundation of your vision.** Without purpose, you're just chasing after things that won't bring you lasting fulfillment.

To start, ask yourself some deep questions:

- **What do I care about?** I mean, really care about. Not the surface-level stuff.
- **What makes me feel alive?** Not just happy, but truly alive.
- **What do I want to contribute to the world?**
- **How do I want to be remembered?**

Don't just gloss over these questions. Sit with them. Reflect. Take your time. **This is the cornerstone of your life vision.**

Once you've got some answers, start pulling everything together. Your vision isn't just about you—it's about the impact you want to have on others. **How do your values align with your unique abilities?** How can you use your skills to contribute to others' well-being?

Here's the thing: **Your vision doesn't need to be grand in the traditional sense.** You don't need to be the next Einstein or Gandhi. Your vision can be as simple as being the best parent you can be, or creating a company that uplifts your community. The key is that it has to **be meaningful** to you. It has to resonate with your core.

3. Practical Steps to Create Your Life Vision

Now let's make this vision practical. You're not going to just daydream about a perfect life. **You're going to make this vision a reality.**

Here's a simple, actionable plan to help you create and bring your life vision to life:

Step 1: Define Your Core Values

What principles guide your life? **What matters most to you?** Your values are the compass that will keep you on track as you pursue your vision. Without values, everything will feel aimless and empty. When you align your life with your values, you are stepping into your authentic self.

Write down your top five values. These might include things like integrity, love, freedom, creativity, or service. These values will act as your guiding principles when tough choices come your way. If your vision and your actions aren't aligned with your values, you'll feel unfulfilled. So, get clear.

Step 2: Visualize Your Ideal Life

Now, get your mind focused. **What does your ideal life look like?** Picture it vividly in your mind. See yourself living out your values, creating your impact. What do you want to be doing five years from now? Ten? This is not about what's realistic right now—it's about *what could be* when you live with intention and vision.

Write down a detailed description of your ideal life. Picture your work, relationships, lifestyle, contributions, and everything else that matters to you. **The more specific you can be, the clearer your vision will be.**

Step 3: Create Actionable Goals

Now, break down your vision into actionable steps. Your life vision is a big picture, but it's made up of smaller pieces. What actions can you take today, tomorrow, and over the next few months to align yourself with this vision?

Set goals that are directly connected to your vision. These should be goals that challenge you, stretch you, and require you to step out of your comfort zone. Don't play small here. You're in the game to win, so **set your sights high**.

Here's a tip: **Focus on the process, not just the outcome.** The guru understands that the journey is just as important as the destination. So don't just set goals for the sake of ticking boxes—set them to grow, evolve, and transform into the person you need to become to live your vision.

Step 4: Commit to Your Vision Daily

Creating a vision is one thing. **Living it every single day is another.** Every day, ask yourself: "What actions am I taking today that bring me closer to my vision?" This is where the real work begins.

Commit to a daily practice that moves you toward your vision. Whether that's through meditation, journaling, learning new skills, or simply reflecting on your values and purpose, consistency is key. **The guru lives with relentless focus**—they don't get distracted by the noise or the shortcuts. They are committed to their mission, no matter how hard it gets.

4. Exercises to Clarify and Align with Your Purpose

It's time to take action. Here are some practical exercises to help you clarify your purpose and align it with your vision:

Exercise 1: The Purpose Discovery Exercise

Sit down with a notebook. Write down answers to the following questions:

- **What do I feel passionate about?**
- **What am I naturally good at?**
- **What would I do for free because it lights me up?**
- **What does the world need right now that I can provide?**

Once you've answered these, look for patterns. The answers to these questions give you the foundation for your life vision. Your purpose is a blend of your passions, strengths, and the world's needs. **Once you recognize it, own it.**

Exercise 2: The Life Vision Statement

Write a statement that outlines your vision for your life. Be as detailed as possible. **Include your goals, values, and the impact you want to have.** This vision should inspire you every time you read it. Let it be a constant reminder of who you're becoming.

Here's an example:

"I am living a life of purpose, serving my community by using my skills to uplift others. I am financially independent, physically healthy, and emotionally grounded. I am constantly growing, learning, and contributing in ways that elevate the world."

Exercise 3: The Goal Alignment Exercise

Once you have your life vision, break it down into actionable goals. Write out specific, measurable, achievable, relevant, and time-bound goals (SMART goals). Then, **look at each goal and ask: "How does this align with my vision?"**

Every single goal should be in service of your larger vision. **If it doesn't fit, let it go.**

Your Life Vision is Waiting for You

You are not here by accident. **Your life has a purpose**—a deep, meaningful mission that will fulfill you and serve others. **It's your job to discover it, to live it, and to align every part of your life with it.**

The guru doesn't wait for a sign. They don't wait for the perfect moment. They take responsibility for creating their life, one conscious choice at a time. **Now it's your turn.**

Get serious. Take action. Create your vision. And then, live it with purpose. **This is your life. Make it count.**

Chapter 6: The Guru's Leadership: Influence Through Example
Part 1: Leadership Beyond Authority

Let me break it down for you. **True leadership is not about barking orders from the top of the mountain or throwing your weight around.** It's not about titles, status, or power. It's not about putting yourself above others. Real leadership—**the kind that leaves a lasting impact**—is about influence, not authority. You don't need a crown or a badge to be a leader. You just need the ability to **show up every day, embody your values, and lead by example.**

The guru understands this. They know that the most powerful leadership doesn't come from wielding control. It comes from living the values you preach and **being the change** you want to see. A guru leads by doing, not by telling. They influence others by **walking the path themselves**—with authenticity, wisdom, and compassion.

If you want to be a true leader, you need to internalize this. **People follow what you do, not what you say.** They'll see your actions before they hear your words. That's the power of leading by example.

1. Authority Is Overrated: Leading with Influence

Authority is easy. Authority is about asserting power. It's about demanding respect and using force to get what you want. But if you want real, lasting influence—**the kind that transforms others and makes a real impact—you need to lead from within. Influence is earned, not given.**

Take a moment to think about the leaders you respect. The ones who really inspired you. **Did they do it by telling you what to do or by showing you how to do it?** Chances are, they didn't need to shout orders. They didn't demand respect. They earned it through their actions.

A guru doesn't use authority to push people around. They use influence to pull people forward. They become a **magnet for others** because they embody the values they espouse. **Their actions speak louder than their words ever could.**

Here's a fact you need to digest: **People want to follow authenticity, not authority.** If you're trying to lead from a place of "I'm the boss," you'll eventually lose your grip. But when you lead from a place of truth, of honesty, and of authenticity, people will follow you no matter what. **You won't have to demand respect; you'll earn it.**

A guru doesn't need to prove their power because they **demonstrate it through how they live.** Their leadership comes from their example, not their position. You don't need a fancy title to lead; you need integrity, clarity, and the ability to inspire others through who you are.

2. Leadership Through Authenticity

Authenticity is the bedrock of effective leadership. **If you want to influence others, you need to be real.** No pretence, no masks. You have to show up as your true self, flaws and all. **People don't follow a fake. They follow someone they can relate to.** You need to embody the values you talk about, live the principles you preach, and show that you're a real person, not some pedestal figure that's impossible to connect with.

A guru is authentic in their leadership. They don't try to project an image of perfection. They acknowledge their imperfections, mistakes, and growth, and they invite others to do the same. **Leadership is about connection, not separation.** You're not on a pedestal above others; you're walking alongside them, showing them what's possible.

When you are authentic, you create an environment where others feel safe to be themselves. You lead by example, showing others that **it's okay to be human.** This type of leadership isn't about being perfect; it's about being transparent. **People follow leaders who show vulnerability, who don't shy away from their humanity.**

Take Gandhi, for example. He didn't lead from a place of authority. He didn't rule through power. He led by walking the talk—by living the principles of non-violence, truth, and compassion every single day. His authenticity was magnetic. **His leadership wasn't about control; it was about inspiring others through his unwavering commitment to truth and justice.**

3. Leadership Through Wisdom

The guru is wise, but wisdom isn't about knowledge—it's about application. **It's about knowing when to speak and when to listen, when to act and when to pause.** Wisdom comes from experience, reflection, and the ability to see the bigger picture. **It's knowing what works and what doesn't, and more importantly, understanding how to use your knowledge to benefit others.**

A guru's leadership isn't based on a show of intellect or fancy words. It's grounded in the wisdom that comes from years of experience, inner work, and deep reflection. **They lead from a place of deep knowing.**

Wisdom also means **being adaptable.** It's not about sticking rigidly to a set of rules but about **understanding when to bend and when to stand firm.** You've got to know your principles, but you also need to be smart enough to adapt to changing circumstances. Wisdom comes from the balance between principle and flexibility.

4. Leadership Through Compassion

Compassion is not just a nice word; it's the heart of effective leadership. **If you want to influence others, you need to care.** Real leaders understand the human experience—they know what it feels like to struggle, to fail, to rise again. A guru doesn't just lead—they serve. **Their leadership is rooted in the ability to empathize with others, to feel their pain, and to support them in their journey.**

Leadership through compassion isn't about saving others—it's about **lifting them up and empowering them to reach their own potential.** You lead by showing others their own greatness, by believing in them when they can't believe in themselves. Compassion means **seeing people for who they are, not for what they can do for you.**

Think of someone like Nelson Mandela. His leadership wasn't about power or dominance; it was about **forgiveness, empathy, and healing.** Even after spending 27 years in prison, he emerged with a heart full of compassion, knowing that his role wasn't just to lead a country, but to heal a divided nation. **Mandela led by example, showing that compassion can overcome even the deepest injustices.**

5. *Actionable Steps: How You Can Lead By Example*

Okay, now that you've got the theory, it's time for you to put it into practice. **Leading by example takes work.** It requires daily commitment and the courage to live your truth, no matter how tough it gets. Here's a no-nonsense guide to start leading by example today:

1. **Get real with yourself.** Stop pretending to be something you're not. Be authentic in everything you do. Show people who you really are—**flaws and all.** People follow authenticity, not perfection.
2. **Live your values.** Don't just talk about integrity, honesty, or compassion—live it every single day. Let your actions reflect your values. **If you say you value something, show it in how you treat others.** If you claim to value health, then start taking care of your body.
3. **Lead with compassion.** Get out of your own head. Focus on serving others, lifting them up, and empowering them to be their best selves. **Ask yourself: How can I help?** not just What can I get?
4. **Share your wisdom.** Don't keep your lessons to yourself. Share what you've learned, not in a preachy way, but in a way that's helpful to others. When people see that you have **wisdom backed by experience**, they'll be drawn to you.
5. **Stay consistent.** Leadership isn't about doing the right thing once or twice. **It's about showing up, day after day, and doing the**

work. If you want to lead by example, you need to live out your principles, even when it's inconvenient or uncomfortable.

6. Lead with Integrity, Not Authority

If you want to lead like a guru, forget the title. Forget the power. **True leadership comes from living your truth, serving others, and leading by example.** Influence is earned, not given. It's about **living with integrity, authenticity, wisdom, and compassion.**

Now, stop sitting on the sidelines. **It's time to lead.** You don't need to wait for permission. You don't need a title or a badge. **You just need to start living the example you want to set.**

Get to it.

Part 2: Building Trust and Connection

———

Listen up. If you want to lead, **you need to earn trust.** Trust isn't something you demand, and it isn't something you get by virtue of a title or a role. **Trust is earned through your actions**—the choices you make every day, the way you show up, and how you follow through. It's the invisible currency of leadership. Without it, your influence is nothing more than smoke and mirrors. **It's flimsy, temporary, and it fades the moment you turn your back.**

A guru understands this better than anyone. **They don't just talk the talk.** They walk the walk. Every single day. And the result? **Deep, lasting connections** built on real trust. This isn't about surface-level niceties. This is about a bond so strong that it can weather storms and withstand the test of time.

But how do you build that trust? How do you get people to believe in you and follow your lead? How do you create connections that last? Well, you do it through **your actions, your integrity, and your unwavering commitment to your values.** That's how you build trust—and that's how you become a leader people can count on.

1. Trust Is Earned Through Consistency

First things first: **trust isn't something you get overnight.** It's not like flipping a switch or signing a contract. Trust is something you **build**—like laying brick after brick until you've built a solid foundation. And the key ingredient in that foundation? **Consistency.**

When you show up day after day, **doing what you say you're going to do,** people notice. When your words match your actions, people start to believe in you. When your values are consistent in every decision you make—no matter how small—the trust others place in you grows. Trust isn't about grand gestures. It's about **doing the little things, consistently, over time.**

If you say you're going to call someone back, you do it. If you promise to meet a deadline, you hit it. If you claim to value honesty, you act with transparency—even when it's uncomfortable. **It's the everyday actions that matter.** And when those actions align with your words, people start to rely on you, to believe in you. Trust is earned, one small action at a time.

2. Be Transparent and Honest

You want to build trust? **Stop hiding.** Stop playing games. **Be transparent. Be honest.** This means showing up as you really are—no masks, no facades. A guru doesn't hide behind a wall of false pretenses. They stand tall, they stand firm, and they let people see them for who they really are.

Here's the deal: people can smell inauthenticity a mile away. They can sense when you're trying to pull one over on them, even if you think you're being slick. **If you want to create a real connection with others, you have to be real with them.** No pretending. No acting like you've got it all figured out. Just honesty.

That doesn't mean you have to air your dirty laundry for the world to see. But it does mean that you should be open, vulnerable, and willing to admit when you don't have the answers. **People trust leaders who are willing to be open about their weaknesses.** When you're transparent, you create space for others to do the same. You lead by example—and that's how trust is built.

Take the Dalai Lama, for example. He's not just a figurehead. He's authentic in everything he does. Whether he's teaching the world about compassion or speaking about his own struggles, he's always **open** and **honest** about his humanity. His transparency creates trust. People believe in him because he **doesn't pretend to be above anyone else.** He shows up, every day, just like you and me. That's powerful. That's leadership.

3. Show Respect for Others

Now, if you think you can build trust without showing respect for the people around you, think again. **Trust and respect go hand-in-hand.** You can't have one without the other. You want people to trust you? **Respect them**

first. When you treat people with respect, you acknowledge their worth, their dignity, and their value. You show that you see them as equals, not as subordinates. **This isn't about hierarchy. It's about human connection.**

A guru treats everyone with respect, regardless of status, position, or title. **They understand that every human being deserves dignity and kindness.** When you treat people with respect, you create a space where others feel comfortable opening up, sharing, and being themselves. They don't feel like they have to hide or pretend to be something they're not. Respect is the foundation of connection—and without that foundation, your relationships will be weak.

One example that comes to mind is Martin Luther King Jr. He didn't just demand respect for himself. He **treated others with deep, unwavering respect**. And in return, people trusted him with their hearts and their lives. They followed him not because he was charismatic, but because he **showed respect to everyone**—even those who disagreed with him.

4. Lead with Empathy

Here's another piece of the puzzle: **empathy. Trust grows when you show that you care about others.** A guru understands this, and they lead with empathy. They take the time to listen to people's concerns, to understand their pain, and to step into their shoes. They don't just hear what others say; they feel it. And when you show that you understand someone's struggles, they'll trust you with their hearts.

Empathy isn't just about listening—it's about **actively engaging with others' emotions and experiences**. It's about showing that you're not just in this for yourself, but that you genuinely care about the well-being of others. When people feel understood and supported, their trust in you deepens.

Think about how **Mother Teresa** led with empathy. She didn't just serve others out of duty; she served them out of love and compassion. She wasn't just helping the poor, the sick, and the marginalized—she was **connecting with them on a deep emotional level.** She made them feel seen, heard, and valued. That's why people trusted her—because she was able to see them in their pain and love them anyway.

5. Practice Integrity and Honor Your Word

Let's talk about integrity. You want to build trust? You need to **be a person of your word.** When you say you're going to do something, you do it. No excuses. No shortcuts. Your integrity is non-negotiable. **You can't build trust if people don't believe you will follow through.** If you want others to respect you and rely on you, you have to show them that you honor your commitments.

Integrity isn't just about big promises; it's about the small ones too. **It's about doing what you say you'll do, even when no one is watching.** It's about living your values in the most mundane, everyday situations. It's about **being the person who always keeps their word, no matter what.**

A guru practices integrity at all times. **They walk their talk.** If they say they value honesty, they'll tell the truth—even when it's difficult. If they promise to support someone, they'll follow through. **People trust leaders who have integrity.** Without it, you have nothing.

6. Actionable Steps to Build Trust and Connection

Now, it's time to put this into action. Trust doesn't happen by accident. You have to work at it, every day. Here's how to start:

1. **Be Consistent.** Show up every day and **do what you say you'll do.** Your actions need to align with your words, and you need to prove yourself through consistent behavior.
2. **Be Transparent.** Don't hide behind a façade. **Be honest** and **open** about who you are and where you stand. When people see you're real, they'll trust you.
3. **Show Respect.** Treat others with dignity and kindness, no matter their status. **Everyone deserves respect**, and you need to give it freely.

4. **Listen with Empathy.** Pay attention to the emotions and struggles of others. **Take time to truly listen** and understand before you offer advice or help.

5. **Honor Your Word.** If you make a commitment, stick to it. **Your integrity is everything.** People will trust you based on how reliably you follow through.

7. Trust is the Foundation of Leadership

If you want to be a leader, stop looking for shortcuts. **Build trust, earn respect, and connect with others through your actions and your values.** Trust isn't given; it's earned. And once you have it, you'll have the kind of influence that lasts. People will follow you not because of your title, but because they know you're someone they can rely on.

Get to work. Build trust. Lead by example.

Part 3: Inspiring Others Through Your Presence

Listen up. This is the truth you need to hear: **The power of a leader is not in what they say, but in who they are when they show up.** It's in your presence. **You lead not with your words, but with your energy, your conviction, and your being.** If you think you can inspire others by just telling them what to do, you're dead wrong. Words are cheap. What people remember is the way you make them feel.

When you walk into a room, people pick up on your vibe before you even open your mouth. **Are you present?** Are you grounded in who you are, clear in your purpose, and unwavering in your integrity? If you're not fully engaged with the moment, you're losing influence. People can sense when a leader is distracted, disinterested, or disconnected from the present moment. **You can't lead from a place of distraction.** If you're not fully committed to the now, you're doing your team, your community, and your mission a disservice.

But when you are fully present—when you are in the moment, connected to the people around you, and anchored in your own truth—something magical happens. You inspire others. You give them permission to do the same. You lead through the sheer force of your presence, and that, my friend, is a game-changer.

1. Presence: The Invisible Force of Leadership

Let me break it down for you. Presence is **energy in motion.** It's the space you create around you with your attention, your focus, and your intention. When you are truly present, people can feel it. **Your energy is contagious.** You've probably seen it happen before: a charismatic leader walks into a room, and suddenly, the atmosphere changes. People stand taller, they lean in, they feel seen. It's as if the leader's very presence commands respect and inspires action.

Think about it: **Have you ever been around someone who is so present, so attuned to the moment, that you couldn't help but be drawn to them?** That's the power of leadership through presence. A guru understands this. They know that they don't need to be the loudest voice in the room to have the greatest impact. **They know that their energy speaks louder than any words they could say.**

One example that comes to mind is Nelson Mandela. When he walked into a room, he didn't have to shout or make grand speeches to get people's attention. **His mere presence was enough to command respect and inspire others to rise to their best.** Whether he was addressing a nation or speaking to a single individual, Mandela radiated a sense of purpose and peace that left an indelible mark on everyone he encountered. That's the power of presence. It doesn't need to be loud—it just needs to be real.

2. Leading by Example: Embodying the Qualities You Want to See

Now, here's where the rubber meets the road: **You cannot inspire others to be what you're not willing to be yourself.** If you want others to show up with integrity, you've got to show up with integrity. If you want others to live with compassion, you've got to live with compassion. **A guru doesn't preach values—they embody them.** They don't ask their followers to do anything they haven't already done themselves.

Here's the truth: **People are always watching.** You think you can just tell people to be patient, to be kind, to be disciplined, and they'll listen? Not a chance. They're watching how you act when you're under pressure. They're watching how you treat others when no one's looking. **Your actions, your attitude, and your energy are what they'll remember.**

Let me give you a personal example. Years ago, I worked with a mentor who embodied everything he taught. He didn't just talk about leadership—he lived it. Every time I saw him, he showed up with clarity, presence, and purpose. It didn't matter if he was talking to a high-level executive or a janitor—he treated everyone with respect. He showed up for his team in the tough moments. He was calm when things were chaotic. **And because of that, he didn't need to say much at all.** His presence did all the work.

A guru isn't looking for followers. A guru is looking for those who are ready to **mirror back the truth that they live every day.** You want people to follow you? Be the embodiment of the values you preach. **The more aligned you are with your core values, the stronger your presence becomes.** When you show up as an example, people don't need to be told what to do—they simply follow your lead.

3. The Art of Being Fully Present in the Moment

There's an art to presence. It's not just about showing up physically, but about being **mentally, emotionally, and spiritually aligned** with the moment. The guru doesn't just stand there, disconnected, while the world goes by. **They are actively engaged with the present.** They listen, they observe, they feel, and they respond.

Here's the problem most people face: They're **too busy** thinking about what's next, what's coming, or what happened in the past. They're constantly in a state of distraction, never fully engaging with the moment at hand. When you're distracted, you can't lead. You're not connected, and neither is anyone else.

You want to inspire others? Start by mastering the art of **being fully present.** Focus on the person in front of you. Listen with your full attention. Respond with intention, not reaction. This is a skill you can cultivate. It starts with awareness, and then it deepens with practice. When you are fully engaged in the moment, people feel it. **They will feel respected, valued, and empowered.**

One simple way to practice presence is through mindfulness. Take a few minutes every day to check in with yourself. **Pause. Breathe. Be still.** Bring your attention back to the here and now. This practice isn't about getting lost in your thoughts; it's about **anchoring yourself in the present moment.** The more you practice being present, the more natural it will become in all aspects of your life. And when you're fully present, people around you can't help but feel inspired.

4. How to Cultivate Presence and Lead by Example

Ready to put this into action? It's time to start developing your presence and **leading by example.** Here are some practical steps to get you started:

1. **Ground Yourself Every Morning.** Begin your day with a moment of mindfulness. Focus on your breath, clear your mind, and align yourself with your purpose. The more you ground yourself, the more present you'll be throughout the day.
2. **Be Fully Engaged in Conversations.** When you talk to someone, give them your full attention. Put down your phone. Look them in the eyes. Listen with your whole being. This is how you build trust and inspire others.
3. **Live Your Values.** Don't just talk about the qualities you want to see in the world—**be them.** If you want people to be compassionate, show compassion. If you want them to be disciplined, demonstrate discipline. Lead with your actions, not your words.
4. **Stay Calm Under Pressure.** When things get tough, **be the calm in the storm.** Your ability to stay grounded and focused will inspire those around you to do the same.
5. **Be Vulnerable.** Don't be afraid to show your humanity. Admit when you don't have all the answers. Share your struggles. Vulnerability creates deep connections, and it makes you more relatable.

5. Presence is Power

If you want to lead, you need to stop focusing on trying to control others or impress them with your words. **Your presence speaks louder than anything you say.** When you're fully present, when you embody the qualities you want to see in the world, you inspire others without ever having to try. People will follow you—not because you told them to, but because they see something in you that they want to emulate.

That's the power of leadership through example. **That's the guru's way.** Now go out and embody it. The world is waiting for you to show up.

Part 4: Leading from Within

———

Listen up. The world doesn't need more leaders who bark orders from the sidelines. What the world needs are leaders who **lead from within**—people who operate from a place of deep authenticity and personal integrity. Leaders who **embody their values** and influence others not through force or manipulation, but by example.

You want to be a real leader? Then stop pretending to be someone you're not. Stop seeking external validation or trying to control everything around you. Leadership isn't about imposing your will on others—it's about being so aligned with your truth that people naturally follow your example. If you want to have real influence, you have to start by leading yourself. It all starts within you.

1. Authentic Leadership: Aligning Your Inner and Outer Worlds

First off, let me make one thing crystal clear: **You cannot fake authentic leadership.** It doesn't matter how much jargon you use, how many books you read, or how many courses you attend—if you're not aligned with who you are at your core, people will see right through it. **Authenticity is the bedrock of leadership.**

Think about it. We've all experienced that one boss or mentor who talks a big game, but their actions don't match their words. You know the one. They say one thing, but they do the exact opposite. **That's not leadership—that's manipulation.** Authentic leadership comes from a place of deep self-awareness. It's about **being congruent** with your beliefs, your actions, and your words.

To lead from within, you've got to look in the mirror and ask yourself: *Do I live by the values I preach?* Are you acting out of fear, ego, or insecurity? Or are you leading with courage, compassion, and clarity? The only way to answer that question honestly is to **take the time to reflect on your values and your actions**.

Here's how you do it:

- **Step 1: Get clear on your values.** What do you stand for? What's non-negotiable for you? Define it in one sentence: *What does integrity mean to you? What does courage look like? What is success in your eyes?*
- **Step 2: Audit your actions.** Look at how you're showing up in the world. Are you practicing what you preach? If not, where's the gap? Find it. Own it.
- **Step 3: Close the gap. Walk your talk.** If you say you're all about integrity, show it in your work and personal life. If you say you believe in collaboration, demonstrate it with your team. **Lead by doing—not by telling others what to do.**

2. Leadership in Action: Listening, Guiding, and Teaching

Now that we've covered the foundation—being real and aligned—it's time to get practical. Real leadership isn't abstract. It's about doing the hard work every day. And that work begins with three core skills: **listening, guiding, and teaching.** These aren't just buzzwords—they're the backbone of leadership that inspires and empowers others. Let's break them down.

Listening: The Foundation of Leadership

The first and most important skill you must master as a leader is **listening.** Don't fool yourself into thinking leadership is about being the loudest or most assertive voice in the room. The greatest leaders are the ones who know how to listen—deeply and attentively.

Why? Because listening is how you understand people's needs, fears, and desires. It's how you build trust and connection. **When you listen without judgment or distraction, you create space for others to share and feel heard.** This is where true leadership begins.

But let's be real: **Most people don't listen.** They're too busy formulating their next response, trying to sound clever, or preparing to get their point across. If you're guilty of this, cut it out. Here's how to really listen:

- **Be fully present.** Put away your phone. Close your laptop. Look the person in the eye. Give them your undivided attention.
- **Don't interrupt.** Hold your impulse to jump in with advice or solutions. **Let them finish first.**
- **Listen with empathy.** Try to understand the person's emotions, not just their words. What are they feeling? What's the deeper message?
- **Ask clarifying questions.** Show them you're engaged by asking questions that encourage deeper conversation. Questions like: *What's most important to you right now?* or *How do you feel about that?*

Guiding: Showing the Way Without Controlling

Once you've mastered listening, the next skill is guiding. **This is where your leadership really takes shape.** You've listened, you've understood, and now it's time to help others move forward. The trick is in guiding people **without controlling them.**

When you try to control someone, you rob them of their autonomy, their creativity, and their sense of self-worth. True leaders **empower people to find their own solutions.** Your job is to guide them to clarity, to help them discover the way forward—not to solve every problem for them.

Here's how to guide effectively:

- **Ask questions that spark self-reflection.** Instead of telling someone what to do, ask them, *What do you think is the best course of action?* or *What resources do you need to move forward?*
- **Encourage ownership.** Give the person space to take responsibility for their decisions. Don't micromanage. Show them

that you trust their judgment.

- **Model behavior.** Lead by example. Demonstrate the values and behaviors you want others to embody. **People learn by watching, not just by listening.**

Teaching: Sharing Knowledge, Not Power

The final piece of the puzzle is **teaching.** As a leader, your role isn't just to inspire action, it's to impart knowledge, skills, and wisdom to those you lead. But make no mistake: teaching isn't about showing off how much you know—it's about helping others learn and grow. **The more you teach, the more you empower others to lead themselves.**

Effective teaching is rooted in simplicity. **Don't complicate things for the sake of sounding smart.** Break down complex concepts into digestible pieces. Give people the tools they need to succeed. Lead them to the answers—not just with your knowledge, but with your ability to help them discover the knowledge within themselves.

Here's how to teach with impact:

- **Start with the basics.** Don't assume people know everything you do. Break down the fundamentals in simple, actionable steps.
- **Use stories and metaphors.** People learn best through stories. Tell them real-life examples, analogies, or metaphors that make complex ideas easy to understand.
- **Be patient.** Understand that teaching takes time. Don't rush the process. Let people ask questions, make mistakes, and grow at their own pace.
- **Offer constructive feedback.** Feedback isn't criticism. It's guidance. When you offer feedback, focus on **growth**, not judgment. Say things like, *Here's what worked well... and here's how you can improve next time.*

3. *Leadership Exercises: Putting It All Into Action*

Now, it's time to take action. **These exercises will help you develop your leadership skills** and start leading from within. Do them. Commit to them. The only way to grow as a leader is to practice.

Exercise 1: The Listening Challenge

Find someone in your life—whether it's a colleague, friend, or family member—and commit to listening to them for 10 minutes without interrupting. **Be fully present.** Ask them open-ended questions. Don't give advice unless they ask for it. Afterward, reflect on how the conversation went. How did you feel? How did they respond?

Exercise 2: The Guiding Exercise

Think of a situation where someone in your life needs guidance. Instead of telling them what to do, ask them questions that help them discover their own solution. **Help them think through their options.** Notice how this feels compared to giving advice or making decisions for them.

Exercise 3: The Teaching Reflection

Take a moment to think about something you're really good at. It could be a skill, a process, or a piece of knowledge you've mastered. Write down the key points and teach it to someone else. **Use stories and metaphors.** Break it down into simple, actionable steps.

4. Lead Yourself, Lead the World

You want to lead? Then **lead yourself first.** Align your inner and outer worlds. Be authentic. Listen. Guide. Teach. **Embodied leadership starts with you.** There's no magic formula. It's about showing up every day, practicing these skills, and refining your approach. Leadership isn't a title. It's a way of being. Lead from within, and others will follow. Simple as that.

Chapter 7: Freedom and Detachment: The Guru's Approach to Letting Go
Part 1: The Illusion of Attachment

Listen up. You're attached to too many things. You hold onto stuff—people, outcomes, ideas—as if they define you. **You think that the more you hold on to, the more secure you'll be.** But I'm here to tell you straight: that's a lie. **Attachment is the root of your suffering,** and until you understand this, you'll keep spinning in circles.

I'm not just talking about material possessions. I'm talking about your attachments to **people's opinions, outcomes, identities, expectations, and your very own past.** Every time you attach yourself to something, you're giving it control over your happiness and well-being. If you don't learn to detach, you'll never know freedom. You'll keep running in place.

1. Attachment Creates Suffering: A Trap of Your Own Making

Let's break this down. Think about something or someone you're attached to. Maybe it's a job. Maybe it's a relationship. Maybe it's an idea of who you think you should be. **Notice how these attachments make you react.** When things don't go as you expect, you get upset, angry, disappointed, or anxious. **Why?** Because you're attached to an outcome. When it doesn't show up the way you've imagined it in your head, it feels like the rug is pulled out from under you.

Attachment traps you. It creates a false sense of security that's built on things outside of you—things you can't control. It's like trying to hold onto sand with an open hand. The tighter you squeeze, the more it slips through your fingers.

When you attach yourself to people's opinions, you lose your power. You'll spend your whole life chasing approval, seeking validation, and getting crushed by criticism. **Your self-worth becomes dependent on others,** and that's a dangerous game to play.

Here's the thing: **Attachment distorts your perception of reality.** It convinces you that what you have, who you're with, and what you've achieved are the only things that matter. But in reality, **everything is temporary.** People come and go. Jobs fade. Bodies age. **The only thing that's permanent is change.** The more you attach, the more you chain yourself to things that will ultimately disappoint you.

2. *The Guru's Ability to Let Go of Attachments*

The guru understands that everything—**everything**—is temporary. A guru doesn't cling to people. They don't cling to possessions, status, or outcomes. **A true guru understands that attachment is a prison, and they are free.** They know that letting go is the key to living with joy, peace, and purpose.

Let me tell you something: A guru isn't some mystical, untouchable figure that floats above it all. They're just people who've figured out one thing—**how to let go.** Let me repeat that. A guru isn't about attachment to ideas or outcomes. **A guru is about being present in the moment, free of expectations.**

You know how they do it? By practicing **detachment.** And no, detachment doesn't mean becoming cold, indifferent, or emotionless. **Detachment means freedom.** It means standing strong in who you are, without being knocked down by external circumstances. It's the ability to move through the world without clinging to things. It's the ability to be involved, but not attached.

3. *How the Guru Lets Go of People, Things, and Outcomes*

A guru's power lies in their ability to **detach from the need for approval,** the desire for success, and the attachment to outcomes. **They don't need people to love them, and they don't need the world to behave a certain way to feel complete.** They show up fully, but they don't let their worth be determined by the reactions of others.

Now, this is key: **Detachment is not abandonment.** A guru does not neglect people or their responsibilities. They give their best, but they do not attach their sense of self-worth or identity to the results. If a student fails, the guru doesn't take it personally. If a relationship ends, they don't fall apart. If their body gets sick, they don't lose their mind. They understand the impermanence of all things, and that understanding **sets them free.**

Imagine, for a second, what it would be like if you could release your attachments. If you didn't rely on external validation to feel good about yourself. **Imagine if you didn't need to control everything in your life to feel safe.** Think about how much energy you'd have, how much room you'd create for growth. When you detach, you can take risks without fear. You can love fully without expectation. You can move through life with ease, knowing that what happens isn't a reflection of your worth.

4. Detachment Doesn't Mean You Don't Care

Here's the misconception that trips people up: **Detachment doesn't mean you stop caring.** It doesn't mean you become apathetic or avoid responsibility. **Detachment means you care deeply, but you're not dependent on anything outside yourself to feel at peace.**

Think of it like this: A gardener cares about their plants, right? But the gardener doesn't *control* the plants. They nurture, water, and guide, but they don't **cling** to the outcome. They don't stress if the plants grow fast or slow. They don't demand perfection. They simply tend to their garden with patience and love, understanding that growth happens in its own time. **That's the essence of detachment.** It's the ability to care deeply while letting go of control.

5. Practical Steps to Letting Go of Attachments

You want to know how to do this? You want to stop being controlled by your attachments? Then you have to put this into practice.

- **Step 1: Identify Your Attachments**

Take a good hard look at your life. What are you attached to? Is it a person? An outcome? A particular result you expect from your work or relationships? Write it down. Get clear. Until you know what you're attached to, you won't be able to let go.

- **Step 2: Ask Yourself Why**

Why are you attached to these things? Why does their presence or absence affect your peace of mind? The answers will give you insight into your fears, insecurities, and needs. **This is where the real work begins.**

- **Step 3: Practice Non-Attachment**

Now that you know your attachments, start practicing detachment. Let go of the need to control. Let go of your expectations. The next time you're faced with a situation where you feel yourself clinging to an outcome, **ask yourself, "Can I be at peace no matter how this turns out?"** Then, let go. Practice it in small moments, like when you're waiting for a response to an email or when your plans get disrupted. **Let go.**

- **Step 4: Embrace Impermanence**

Remember, nothing is permanent. People change. Jobs come and go. Possessions wear out. **Everything is in constant flux.** Once you accept this, you'll stop attaching your happiness to things that will inevitably fade.

- **Step 5: Be Present**

Focus on the present moment. Attachments thrive when you're not present. They pull you into the past (regret, nostalgia) or push you into the future (anxiety, fear). The more you practice being present, the less power your attachments will have over you.

6. *The Power of Letting Go: Living with Freedom*

You want freedom? **Let go.** Stop holding on to everything that weighs you down. **Let go of your need for certainty, approval, and control.** Let go of your old identity, your past mistakes, your wounds. **Let go of everything that's not serving your highest purpose.**

When you let go, you create space for something better—**for growth, for peace, for love.** The guru's life is a life of freedom because they've learned to detach. You can do the same. It's your choice.

Now, get moving. Let go of what you're holding onto.

Part 2: The Freedom of Non-Resistance

———

Listen up. **Resistance is your enemy. Every time you push back against life, you make it harder on yourself.** The world is constantly shifting—change is the only thing you can count on—and yet, you're out there trying to control it, fight it, shape it to your will. **And that's why you're suffering.**

You think you can control the waves in the ocean. **You can't.** But you can learn how to surf them. **That's what the guru does.** The guru knows that resistance is pointless. They don't waste energy fighting what is. **They've mastered the art of non-resistance.**

You don't have to be a guru to understand this. **You don't need some secret power.** All you need is to get out of your own damn way. **Stop resisting.**

1. The Power of Acceptance and Surrender

You want freedom? Then accept what is. **Acceptance is the key. Surrendering to what is doesn't mean you're weak or passive.** It means you stop fighting against reality. **It means you stop trying to impose your will on everything around you.**

It's time to stop acting like you're in control of the universe. **You're not.** The world doesn't revolve around you. **Life doesn't owe you anything.** Things happen, whether you like them or not. **Resistance only makes them worse.** It's like running into a brick wall and then yelling at the wall for being there. What do you think is going to happen? **You'll just hurt yourself more.**

Here's the truth: **What you resist, persists.** The more you push against something—whether it's a feeling, a person, or a situation—the stronger it becomes in your life. The harder you try to control the flow of life, the more you get pulled under by it. But when you stop fighting, when you stop clinging to your idea of how things should be, **you open the door to real freedom.**

2. *The Guru's Approach to Acceptance*

The guru doesn't try to resist life. They don't get angry when things don't go their way. **They accept the moment, exactly as it is.** And this acceptance doesn't come from a place of resignation or passivity—it comes from profound understanding.

The guru knows this: **You can't change the present moment.** Whatever is happening right now, it's already here. Whether it's a person, an event, or an emotion—**it's here.** The only choice you have is how you respond. You can fight it, or you can surrender to it. And here's the secret—**surrender is where the power lies.**

The guru doesn't resist pain. They don't resist discomfort. They don't resist frustration, anger, or even fear. **They feel those things fully and completely**—but they don't cling to them. **They allow them to pass.**

Let's take a real-world example: Think about a difficult conversation you're avoiding. Maybe it's a conversation with a boss, a spouse, or a friend. You're resisting it because you're afraid of the outcome. **You're trying to control the situation, trying to predict what will happen, and worrying about what people will think.** You're creating stress in your body and mind. You're tightening up, resisting, and in that resistance, you're making the situation worse.

What would happen if you just accepted that the conversation is going to happen, no matter what? **What if you surrendered to the moment instead of fighting it?** What if you simply showed up, present and open, without any attachment to the outcome?

Here's the kicker: When you stop resisting, things unfold naturally. The world stops pushing back. **Life becomes easier, lighter, and more fluid.**

3. *How Non-Resistance Transforms Your Life*

Non-resistance isn't about giving up or doing nothing. **It's about recognizing that control is an illusion**—and then choosing to act with awareness and clarity. The guru understands this. They don't waste energy resisting or pushing against the tide. They flow with it.

Think about the last time you were stuck in traffic. What did you do? Did you resist? Did you get angry, curse, and fume at the situation? **Did it make the traffic go faster?** No. But you wasted energy in that resistance. You created stress in your body and mind, and you made your experience worse.

Now, imagine you're in the same traffic jam—but this time, you don't resist. **You accept it.** You listen to a podcast, maybe you breathe deeply, or you just enjoy the stillness. Suddenly, the situation is more bearable. You're not fighting it. You're simply in it. And because of that, you can stay calm, stay focused, and stay in control of your internal state.

Non-resistance transforms your inner experience. **You stop creating unnecessary stress.** Instead of being consumed by frustration or fear, you start seeing the bigger picture. **You start moving through life with more peace, more grace.** You begin to respond to life instead of reacting.

4. Practical Steps to Cultivate Non-Resistance

Okay, let's get down to business. You want to apply this to your life? You want to stop fighting and start flowing? Then here's what you need to do:

Step 1: Recognize Your Resistance

The first step is awareness. You can't let go of resistance if you're not aware of it. **Start noticing when you're fighting.** When do you feel tension in your body? When do you feel yourself bracing for impact? It could be in a conversation, a work situation, or even when you're waiting for something to happen. **Pay attention to where you're holding on.**

Step 2: Stop Fighting the Present Moment

Once you recognize where you're resisting, your next step is to stop fighting it. This isn't about letting people walk all over you or accepting behavior you don't agree with. It's about **accepting the reality of the moment without trying to control it.**

So, when something happens that triggers you, instead of getting caught up in the emotions of the situation, **breathe.** Step back. Look at it objectively. Ask yourself, "What's here right now?" And then **accept it.**

Step 3: Shift Your Perspective

Here's the kicker—**non-resistance is about perspective.** Instead of seeing challenges as obstacles, see them as opportunities to learn, grow, and evolve. This shift in mindset will free you from the need to control the outcome of every situation.

Step 4: Let Go of the Need for Certainty

You can't control everything, and you'll never know exactly what will happen next. **The more you try to predict and control every little detail of your life, the more you bind yourself to fear and anxiety.** The guru knows this. They trust that everything will unfold as it should.

Let go of the need to have it all figured out. Trust in the process, even if it doesn't make sense at first. **Life has a way of working itself out, often in ways you can't predict or understand.**

5. *The Freedom of Non-Resistance: A Life Without Stress*

The moment you stop resisting, you enter the realm of freedom. **You stop living in reaction to life,** and you start living with intention. You stop fighting against your circumstances and start **responding with wisdom and clarity.**

The guru's freedom isn't in what they have or what they've achieved—it's in their ability to flow with life, to **accept the moment as it is** without attachment or resistance.

Now, it's your turn. **Stop fighting.** Stop trying to control. **Accept what is. Surrender to the flow.**

When you do, you'll discover that freedom isn't something you need to attain. It's something you already have—it's simply the freedom to be exactly who you are, right now.

Stop resisting. **Start living.**

Part 3: Detachment from Ego

———

Alright, listen up. **Ego is the enemy.** It's the thing that keeps you trapped in the cycle of suffering. It's the thing that tells you who you are, what you want, and what you need. It creates stories about you—**false stories**—and then it locks you into them. And those stories? **They don't serve you.**

The ego is a construct—a set of beliefs and patterns that you've picked up over the years. **It's not you.** But because you identify with it, because you think that's who you are, it dictates how you act, how you feel, and how you see the world. **It keeps you small.** It keeps you trapped in the past and afraid of the future.

A guru doesn't let the ego control them. **A true guru knows: You are not the ego.** The guru has learned to detach from it—to see it for what it is: a mask, a role, a fleeting illusion. **You can do the same.**

1. Understanding How the Ego Binds Us to False Identities

Here's the hard truth: **Your ego is a liar.** It tells you that you are your job, your status, your achievements, your relationships, your body, your opinions, your emotions—anything that's temporary and fleeting. **It feeds you a story** about who you are, and you buy into it, hook, line, and sinker. But here's the kicker—**the more you identify with the ego, the less you understand who you truly are.**

The ego thrives on separation. It's the part of you that compares. It says, "I am better than you, worse than you, richer than you, smarter than you." **The ego is always creating divisions**—divisions between you and others, between you and your higher self, between you and the present moment.

Let me put it in perspective. **You've probably had the experience of getting attached to a label.** Maybe it's "I'm the successful entrepreneur," "I'm the artist," "I'm the kind, compassionate person." Whatever label you cling to, **that's the ego at work.** And the problem with labels is they limit you. They restrict who you can be and what you can experience. The guru knows that labels are prisons. **They don't define us.** They are temporary markers that we attach ourselves to in order to feel secure. But in reality? **They're just stories.**

When you cling to your ego identity, you keep yourself locked in a narrow narrative. **You prevent yourself from evolving, growing, and stepping into your full potential.** The guru isn't defined by any one identity—they're fluid, adaptable, always changing. **They know they are more than just one story.**

2. Practices for Disidentifying from Ego-Based Thoughts and Behaviors

If you want to break free from the grip of the ego, **it's going to take some work.** But the good news? You don't need some mystical power. You don't need to retreat to a mountaintop. What you need is to practice the art of detachment. Here are some practical exercises to help you do that:

Step 1: Observe the Ego, Don't Identify with It

The first step in detaching from the ego is to start observing it without getting sucked in. **When you feel triggered, when you feel that strong reaction—stop.** Watch it. Watch what the ego is doing in your mind. **Notice the judgments, the comparisons, the stories.** You'll catch yourself thinking, "I can't believe he said that to me," or "I have to prove I'm right." But here's the key: **Don't buy into it.**

Instead of getting caught up in the narrative, **step back.** Be the observer, not the participant. Just because a thought comes into your head doesn't mean it's true. **The ego is always talking.** But you don't have to listen. **You can choose not to engage.** When you detach from the thought, you detach from the ego.

Step 2: Question Your Stories

You want to break free from the ego's grip? **Start questioning your stories.** Ask yourself: "Is this thought really who I am? Is this belief really serving me?" You've got a story about being "too shy," or "not good enough," or "always failing"—but **who told you that story?** Who gave you that narrative?

The guru knows that all the stories you've been telling yourself about your identity are just **the past trying to define the future.** They're stories you've adopted along the way, but they're not the truth of who you are. **You are not your story.** Question it. Break it down. Ask yourself: **"Who would I be if I stopped believing this?"**

Step 3: Practice Non-Identification with Labels

Stop identifying with your labels. **You are not your job.** You are not your bank balance. You are not your relationships. You are not your achievements. When you identify with any one of these labels, you trap yourself in a limited version of who you are. **You become attached to the story, and that story will inevitably fall apart.**

The guru doesn't cling to labels. They don't let their worth be defined by external circumstances. **The guru's identity is not tied to the ego.** Their true nature is infinite, boundless, beyond form. And guess what? **That's your true nature, too.**

Take a moment and ask yourself: **"Who am I, without the labels?"** Without the job title, the family role, the accomplishments, the failures. Just you, as you are. No story. No identity. Just being.

Step 4: Practice Detachment in Everyday Life

You can't just meditate your way out of ego attachment. You've got to practice it in real life. **In the moment.** When someone cuts you off in traffic, or when someone criticizes you at work—how do you react? The ego wants to defend itself, argue back, prove it's right. **But the guru doesn't need to prove anything.**

When you face these situations, practice **detachment**. Step back. **Don't respond from the ego's place of defense or attack.** Instead, respond from the place of wisdom and awareness. When you don't take things personally, when you don't attach to the opinions of others, **you free yourself from the ego's grip.**

Step 5: Meditate on Emptiness and Non-Self

Here's where the real magic happens. **Meditation is the tool of the guru.** It's the way they detach from the ego. But don't just meditate on calmness or peace—meditate on **emptiness**. Meditate on **non-self.**

Sit quietly and reflect on the idea that **you are not your thoughts, you are not your body, you are not your past, you are not your future.** When you meditate on non-self, you begin to experience the truth: You are simply awareness. The ego isn't you. It's a temporary construct. The real you is boundless, timeless, formless.

Meditate on that. Sit in the silence and let the ego dissolve. **Feel the freedom in that space.**

3. Embracing the Freedom of Detachment from Ego

Here's the bottom line: **Detachment from the ego is the key to freedom.** When you stop identifying with the stories, the roles, and the labels, you step into your true power. You become unshakable, unstoppable. The world doesn't control you anymore. **You control your response to the world.**

The guru understands this freedom intimately. **They live beyond the ego.** They have disidentified with the false self. And when you follow their example, when you practice these steps, **you can live beyond the ego too.**

It's time to stop identifying with everything that's not truly you. **Let go of the stories. Let go of the labels.** Let go of the ego's grip on your life. **Step into your true self—the one that is infinite, free, and untouchable.**

Are you ready to let go of the false self? Are you ready to break free from the ego? **Then start now.** The moment you choose detachment, you choose freedom. And there's no going back.

Part 4: Cultivating Freedom in Daily Life

L et's be clear: **Detachment doesn't mean checking out of life.** It doesn't mean avoiding relationships, abandoning responsibility, or retreating into a cave somewhere. No, detachment is **freedom in action.** It's about letting go of all the things that weigh you down—attachments, fears, past hurts, and expectations—and staying present in the moment, fully engaged with life **as it is.**

I don't want to hear any more of this "I can't let go" or "It's too hard." **If you're serious about your growth, you need to understand something—detachment is not a luxury.** It's a necessity. The more you hold on to things, the more you carry around baggage. And let me tell you, that baggage? **It's slowing you down.** If you want to be a true leader, a modern guru, you've got to let go. Let go of the past. Let go of expectations. Let go of anything that pulls you away from the present.

If you're not willing to do that, don't bother reading further. But if you're ready, if you're serious, then keep reading, and let's get to work.

1. Exercises for Letting Go of Attachments

You want to live free? Then it starts with practice. **Detachment is a muscle**—you have to train it every day. You want a clear path forward? Then stop carrying the past with you. Stop dragging it along like dead weight.

Here are some practical, no-nonsense exercises to help you start letting go. **Do them. And do them now.**

Exercise 1: Inventory Your Attachments

First step: take stock. You can't let go of something you're not even aware you're attached to. **Grab a pen and paper.** Write down everything in your life you feel attached to—your possessions, your relationships, your job, your image, your opinions, your fears, your desires.

Don't hold back. Write it all down. These are the things that control you. These are the things you hold onto out of fear, insecurity, or pride.

Now, look at the list. What's holding you back? What's keeping you stuck? **Be honest.** Is that car, that job title, that need to always be right, really serving you? Or is it just a crutch, a distraction from your true potential?

After you've written the list, **cross out the things that no longer serve you.** You know which ones they are. The relationships that drain you. The habits that keep you small. The stuff you hoard just to feel important.

Take a moment. **Get clear on your attachments**—only when you're clear can you start letting go.

Exercise 2: The Letting Go Ritual

Now that you've identified your attachments, it's time to get serious. You're going to have to release them. This isn't just some fluffy meditation exercise. **This is a mental and emotional process,** so treat it as such.

Find a quiet space. Sit comfortably. Close your eyes. **Focus on your breath.** As you breathe in and out, start picturing the attachments on your list. One by one, imagine letting go of them. See them in your mind's eye and slowly, deliberately, release them. You can imagine them floating away, or disintegrating, or dissolving into thin air.

Feel the freedom in your body. Feel the weight lifting. As each attachment releases, breathe in deeper, letting more space into your life.

Now, here's the real test: after you've done this exercise, go about your day. **Notice what happens when the attachments try to pull you back in.** Someone challenges your opinion, or you feel the need to prove yourself, or that fear of failure creeps in. **Catch it.** You're not weak for feeling attached—you're just human. But you have the power to notice it, and **to let it go again.**

The key here is practice. The more you practice releasing attachments, the easier it becomes. **You'll start to realize just how much of your life is spent holding on to things that don't matter.**

Exercise 3: Practice Non-Attachment in Relationships

Now, let's talk about your relationships. **This is the hardest one for most people.** But I'll tell you right now: it's the most important.

You can't control people. You can't control how others act, how they feel, or what they think. So why do you keep trying? **Let go of the need to control others.**

I'm not saying you should stop caring about people or stop being compassionate. Far from it. **But you need to stop clinging.** Stop relying on people to validate you. Stop attaching your happiness to their approval or behavior.

Next time you interact with someone, practice non-attachment. **Be present.** Listen. Don't think about what they can do for you. Don't think about how they'll react to your words. Just be there with them, without any strings attached. Don't manipulate the situation to get something for yourself. Give, without expecting anything in return.

Let go of the need to have things go your way. And you'll see, **relationships will become deeper, more authentic.** When you stop grasping, you make space for true connection.

2. Integrating Detachment and Freedom into Your Personal Life

Now, here's the thing: **detachment is not a one-off exercise.** This isn't something you do for an hour and then forget about it. It's a mindset. **It's a way of living.**

To integrate detachment into your daily life, here's what you need to do:

1. Practice Presence

When you're with someone, be with them. When you're doing something, do it. Don't be half in, half out. **Drop the distractions.** The guru is always present, always aware of the moment. **So should you be.**

Focus on the here and now. **If you're eating, eat. If you're walking, walk.** Don't worry about the future. Don't regret the past. Be where your feet are, because that's where your power is. The moment you stop trying to control everything, stop chasing outcomes, you free yourself.

2. Let Go of Expectations

Expectations will always keep you bound. If you expect people to behave a certain way or for life to go according to plan, **you're setting yourself up for disappointment.** Expectations are just another form of attachment.

I'll tell you this: the guru **expects nothing** and accepts everything. They don't cling to any one outcome. They understand that life is dynamic, unpredictable, and constantly changing. **And they're okay with that.**

Next time you set out to do something, let go of any expectation of what the result should be. **Just act with integrity, give it your best, and let the chips fall where they may.**

3. Let Go of the "Need" for Approval

One of the biggest traps people fall into is the need for validation. **Stop needing approval from others to feel good about yourself.**

Do you know how many people stay stuck in jobs or relationships because they're looking for someone else's approval? **You've got to break that cycle.** The guru doesn't wait for others to say they're worthy. They know their worth doesn't come from external validation.

So here's what I'm asking you: **Let go of needing others to approve of your choices.** Make decisions that align with your true values, not with what others think is best. The moment you stop seeking approval is the moment you unlock true freedom.

3. Final Thoughts: Detachment Equals Freedom

Detachment isn't about withdrawing from the world. **It's about engaging with life without getting caught up in it.** It's about being present, giving without expectation, and acting without attachment.

By practicing detachment, you free yourself from the constant cycle of wanting, needing, and striving. **You step into your true power.** You become a force of nature, unstoppable because you're no longer chained to anything that doesn't serve you.

The key to living like a guru is living in the world, **but not being of it.** So get out there and start practicing. Let go. Breathe. And watch how much lighter you feel.

You've got this. Now, let go.

Chapter 8: The Guru's Spiritual Wisdom: Balancing the Inner and Outer Worlds
Part 1: Understanding Spiritual Wisdom

———

Alright, listen up. I don't care if you've been meditating for five years or five minutes—**spiritual wisdom is not some abstract concept** for you to nod along to while sitting in a lotus position. **It's real.** It's something you can *live*. Spiritual wisdom is about **doing the work**, facing the tough stuff, and integrating what you've learned into every decision, every relationship, every moment.

But here's the kicker: **spiritual wisdom doesn't belong to any one person, tradition, or philosophy.** There's no exclusive club for those who know the "right" way. It's universal. **It's a collection of truths and principles** that, when you strip away the fluff, resonate across all spiritual traditions. They're the same principles that have been guiding sages, gurus, and great leaders for millennia.

You don't need to reinvent the wheel. All you need is the ability to **take what's useful** and apply it to your life. And that's exactly what I'm going to teach you here.

1. Spiritual Teachings Across Traditions: What's the Common Thread?

If you've been paying attention, you've heard the same messages over and over again. They come from Buddhism, Christianity, Sufism, Hinduism, Taoism, and even modern psychology. But here's the thing: **they're all saying the same thing**—they just dress it up in different clothes.

Here's what you need to know:

- **Detachment and letting go:** From the Buddha to the Bhagavad

Gita, the same core idea exists. You need to detach from your ego, from your desires, from the illusion of control. Why? Because **attachment leads to suffering.** Period.

- **Being present and aware:** The concept of mindfulness is not new. It's as old as humanity. It shows up in Zen teachings, it shows up in Christian mysticism, it shows up in the Tao. **To live fully, you must be aware.** You've got to pay attention. You can't be stuck in the past or in the future. You can only act in the present moment, and the only way to do that is to be **fully here, right now.**

- **The interconnectedness of all things:** Whether it's the idea of oneness in Hinduism, the unity of all things in Taoism, or the "kingdom of God" in Christianity, the essence of reality is the same. **Everything is connected.** The guru knows this and lives this truth. When you see yourself as part of the whole, your actions shift. You stop seeing life as a battleground and start seeing it as a field to work in harmony with.

- **The path of selfless service:** The most repeated message across all traditions is that true spiritual growth comes through service. Whether it's the concept of *seva* in Hinduism or the idea of "loving your neighbor" in Christianity, **selfless service is a central practice.** The more you give to others without expecting anything in return, the more you open yourself up to the wisdom of the universe.

Now here's the deal—**you don't have to subscribe to any one tradition** to live these principles. They're universal truths that transcend religion. **The guru doesn't get bogged down by labels.** They don't need to identify as Buddhist, Christian, or anything else. They simply live the truth of what they know and experience, day in and day out.

2. How Gurus Use Universal Wisdom to Guide Their Lives and Others

THINK LIKE A MODERN GURU

The guru is not some mystical figure up in the Himalayas, sitting on a throne of enlightenment, waiting for the world to catch up. **No.** The guru is **you, in action**. The guru is a person who lives out the truth of universal wisdom through their every decision, every action, and every thought. They're not perfect, they're human—but they're committed to living with awareness, responsibility, and humility.

Let's break it down:

1. Living with Purpose and Intent

Gurus live with **purpose**. They are laser-focused on their mission: to spread love, peace, and wisdom. But this doesn't mean they're rigid or inflexible. **Purpose is not a straight line—it's a way of being**. It's a compass, guiding every action. And the guru knows this. Whether it's a simple act like helping someone cross the street or guiding someone through a difficult spiritual dilemma, the guru is always operating with purpose.

You want to be like a guru? You need to get clear on your own purpose. And let me make it clear: **purpose is not something you "find"—it's something you *create*.** Start by asking yourself, "What am I committed to in this moment?" If you're not clear, you're just drifting. And that's not the way to lead your life or guide others.

2. The Art of Letting Go: The Guru's Secret to Freedom

Here's the deal: **Letting go is the core of spiritual wisdom.** It's not just some catchy phrase to post on your Instagram story. It's the foundation. When you let go, you let go of the past, of your expectations, of your ego, and of your need for control.

Think about this: The more you try to control something, the more it controls you. When you try to **hold on tightly**, you suffocate life's natural flow. This is true in relationships, in your career, in your physical possessions, and even in your own mind. **The guru knows how to let go.** They don't resist what is; they don't cling to what was. They know that **life is fluid**, and they don't fight it.

You're not a guru if you're busy fighting the tide. The guru lets go, moves with the current, and directs the flow with intent. The moment you start trying to manipulate the world, you lose your connection to wisdom. The guru stays connected by practicing **non-resistance**.

3. Seeing Beyond Dualities: The Guru's Approach to Life's Contradictions

Most people see life in dualities—good/bad, right/wrong, success/failure. The guru sees beyond these superficial distinctions. **They see the world as it truly is: a spectrum.** There's no "black and white"—there are infinite shades of gray, and the guru embraces them all.

If you're locked into rigid thinking, you're trapped. **You're limiting yourself.** You think you can't change because you see yourself as a failure, or you think you can't move forward because your path didn't look the way you expected it to. But the guru understands that **everything is impermanent.** Every situation, every circumstance, is a chance to grow. Life is fluid. And the guru's wisdom comes from embracing that flow.

4. Teaching Through Example, Not Words

Now, let's talk about the most important part of being a guru: **leading by example.** The guru doesn't need to preach from a pedestal. They don't need to talk about how enlightened they are or tell people what to do. **Their life speaks for itself.** They live in accordance with universal wisdom, and that's the lesson. When you live this truth, people will be drawn to you, and they will learn from your example.

You want to influence others? **Be the example.** Be the embodiment of the wisdom you seek to teach. People will see the change in you, and they'll ask you what your secret is. And then, when they ask, you'll be able to say: **It's not a secret. It's a practice.**

Final Thoughts: Spiritual Wisdom is Practical

Spiritual wisdom isn't some abstract, unreachable ideal. It's **practical, everyday knowledge** that you can apply to every single part of your life. It's not about how much you can memorize or how many books you read. It's about how much you can **live**.

Remember: The guru is not a person who knows everything. **The guru is the person who knows how to stay present, how to serve others, and how to let go.** When you start living like this, you'll begin to realize that **spiritual wisdom isn't something you find—it's something you create.** You live it every day.

Now, get out there and start practicing. It's time to integrate this wisdom. It's time to live it. **The world needs more gurus.** Start with yourself.

Part 2: Integrating the Inner and Outer Worlds

Alright, time to stop pretending. **You can't separate the inner world from the outer world.** You can't hide in a cave and hope the world will change, and you can't act like a self-righteous savior trying to change everything without first getting your inner house in order. You want to make a real difference? **Start by looking inside.**

You've heard it before: "Inner peace is everything." But let me tell you something: **Inner peace alone is not enough.** It's great to feel serene, calm, and centered. It's wonderful to meditate, to breathe deeply, to connect with your higher self. But the real power comes when you take that inner peace, that quiet knowing, and channel it into action. **Because action is the bridge between who you are and who you want to be.**

So, let's get this straight: **Inner peace without action is stagnation.** And action without inner peace? Chaos.

This chapter is about **finding the balance**—how to live from a place of inner clarity, strength, and calm, while also taking the necessary actions in the world to create change, fulfill your purpose, and make a real impact.

1. The Relationship Between Inner Peace and Outer Action

Let's break this down into something you can actually use. Here's the truth:

- **Inner peace is your foundation.** Without it, everything you try to build on top will collapse. Your mind will be scattered, your energy depleted, and your purpose unclear. The people around you will sense this instability. **Inner peace gives you the strength to act from a place of wisdom.** You're not acting out of fear, insecurity, or reaction—you're acting from clarity.
- **Outer action is your expression.** It's how you bring your inner

peace into the world. It's how you fulfill your purpose. But if you try to act without inner peace, **you'll be like a headless chicken running around in circles**—you'll burn yourself out, make rash decisions, and eventually become frustrated. **Action without inner peace lacks focus and effectiveness.**

The guru knows this. The guru isn't some passive observer of life. **They act.** They lead. They engage with the world. But their actions are aligned with their inner state. They don't react to circumstances—they respond. They don't make decisions from a place of fear—they make them from clarity. They **integrate the inner with the outer** seamlessly, and they do it with purpose and intention.

2. *The Inner-Outer Reflection: How the External World Mirrors Your Inner World*

Here's a concept you need to get **deep in your bones: The external world is a reflection of your inner consciousness.** Let me say that again: *The world you see outside of you is a reflection of what's inside of you.*

Think about it. If you're constantly anxious, angry, or fearful, you'll see the world as a dangerous, threatening place. You'll interpret everything through that lens—your relationships will feel tense, your work will feel like a struggle, and you'll constantly be in a defensive mode. **Why? Because you're projecting your inner state outward.**

Now, let me flip that around: When you cultivate inner peace, clarity, and compassion, the world starts to look different. You'll see opportunities instead of obstacles. You'll find solutions where others see problems. You'll attract people who align with your energy, people who lift you up. The world becomes a reflection of your inner growth.

The guru understands this deeply. They don't waste time blaming the world for their problems. They **look inward** and say, "What part of me needs to change?" They know that the universe mirrors their consciousness, so if they want to change their reality, they need to change their mind.

3. Practical Steps for Integrating the Inner and Outer Worlds

It's all well and good to talk about inner peace and universal reflection, but you're here to **do something** with this knowledge. So let's get to work. Here's how to integrate the inner and outer worlds in a practical way:

Step 1: Start with Self-Awareness

Before you can act with clarity, you need to know what's going on inside. **Self-awareness is key.** You can't fix what you don't acknowledge.

- **Exercise:** For the next seven days, do a daily "check-in" with yourself. Set aside five minutes every morning or evening to ask yourself:
    - "How am I feeling right now?"
    - "What's going on in my mind?"
    - "What do I need to address today?"
    - "What part of me is resisting life right now?"

Be brutally honest with yourself. This isn't about making excuses. This is about acknowledging what's real, so you can move from a place of awareness.

Step 2: Cultivate Inner Peace Daily

You want to act in the world? Then you need to **be solid inside**. Period. Whether it's meditation, journaling, walking in nature, or breathing exercises—**do whatever it takes to ground yourself daily**. A guru doesn't wait for peace to "magically" show up—they **create it**.

- **Exercise:** Choose one daily practice that helps you center yourself. Do it every day. Start small, but commit to it. Meditation, breathwork, even just five minutes of silence—whatever helps you come back to the present moment and connect to your inner self.

Step 3: Take Aligned Action

Once you've got your inner foundation in place, it's time to **act**. And the key here is to act from a place of alignment. That means you don't just do what's on your to-do list—you **act with purpose**.

- **Exercise:** Before each action or decision, ask yourself:
  - "Am I doing this because it aligns with my values and my purpose?"
  - "Does this decision reflect the clarity I've gained from my inner practice?"
  - "Is this action serving the highest good of everyone involved?"

If the answer is no, don't do it. If the answer is yes, step forward with confidence.

Step 4: Observe and Adjust

Here's where most people fail—they take one action, see a result, and think they're done. Wrong. **The process of integration is continuous.** You're constantly observing, adjusting, and recalibrating.

- **Exercise:** After every action, take a moment to reflect:
  - "How did I feel during this action?"
  - "Was my mind at peace while I did this?"
  - "What can I learn from this experience to improve next time?"

Make sure you're constantly growing and evolving.

4. The Guru's Role in the World: Action from a Place of Peace

Let's talk about the guru's role here. The guru isn't some passive, detached monk. The guru is **fully engaged** in life. They take action, they make decisions, they take on responsibility. They serve the world, but **they do it from a place of inner clarity and peace.**

The guru knows that if they want to impact the world, they must first **master themselves**. They can't pour from an empty cup. They can't heal the world if they're still broken inside. So, the guru takes time to cultivate inner peace, but then they use that peace to **act in the world**—and they do so with wisdom, compassion, and responsibility.

5. Final Takeaway: Integrate, Don't Isolate

You can't separate the inner from the outer. They're not two separate worlds—they're **interconnected**. Your inner state determines the actions you take, and your actions determine how the world reflects back to you.

If you want to make a difference, it's not enough to meditate in isolation. **Get out there. Take action.** Be in the world—but always be rooted in your inner peace. Act with clarity. Live with purpose. And let your life be the example of the integration of inner wisdom and outer action.

Now go. Live it. The world needs you—fully aligned, fully present, fully powerful.

Part 3: Living with Integrity

———

Listen up. Integrity isn't some nice-to-have quality—it's the **foundation** of everything you do. **If you don't have integrity, you've got nothing.** It doesn't matter how many mantras you chant, how much meditation you do, or how many spiritual books you read. Without integrity, your inner and outer worlds will always be out of sync. It's as simple as that.

Let's cut through the fluff. Integrity means that what you say, what you do, and what you believe all **align.** There's no division between your words and your actions. There's no conflict between what you think you should be doing and what you actually do. **If you say you're committed, you act committed. If you say you value honesty, you are honest.** No exceptions.

Now, you might be thinking: "Sure, sounds good. But how do I do that in the real world?" Good question. Because if you think integrity is some abstract concept for gurus to preach about, **you've got another thing coming.** Integrity is the hardest thing to live by, and it's where the rubber meets the road. It's easy to say you've got high values when things are easy. But when the pressure's on, when your ego's on the line, that's when integrity is tested. And that's when it matters most.

So, let's break it down. I'm going to show you what integrity really means in both your spiritual and material life, and how to walk that path like a true guru. Ready? Let's dive in.

1. The Role of Integrity in Spiritual and Material Life

Most people think of spirituality as something **ethereal, disconnected from the real world.** They think of a guru as someone who spends their time sitting cross-legged on a mountaintop, meditating in a lotus position, free from the troubles of daily life. Wrong. The guru is **deeply rooted in reality.** They're not avoiding the world—they're engaged with it, fully and consciously. **That's where the power of integrity lies.**

Here's the deal: **Integrity isn't just about being honest in your spiritual practice—it's about being honest in every area of your life.** It's about living authentically across all spheres: in your work, relationships, finances, health, and even your entertainment. When you live with integrity, there's no disconnect between your spiritual beliefs and your daily actions. They **work together**. What you believe shapes what you do, and what you do reinforces what you believe.

Spirituality and materialism are not opposites. They're **two sides of the same coin.** You can't hide behind some lofty spiritual ideals if you're failing to show up in the material world. It's one thing to chant about peace and love—it's another thing to actually practice it when your boss yells at you, when your partner challenges you, or when you don't get what you want.

You see, integrity is **what keeps you grounded** in both realms. It allows you to walk the path between the inner world of consciousness and the outer world of action. **It's the glue that holds everything together.**

2. The Guru's Path of Living Authentically and Consistently

So, you want to live like a guru? You want to walk the path of spiritual wisdom and material success? Then understand this: **The guru is unwavering in their authenticity.** There's no double life. They don't act one way in public and another in private. Their **actions speak louder than their words** because they live with the absolute certainty that their behavior reflects their beliefs.

To live authentically means that you're the same person in every situation. You don't switch between different masks depending on who you're with. You don't pretend to be spiritual when you're around spiritual people, and then go back to being a jerk when you're around people who don't share your values. **Your life is your message.** What you do in the quiet of your own home is just as important as what you do in front of a crowd.

A guru's integrity isn't something they put on for show. It's **what they breathe**. They live it. They eat it. They sleep it. And that's why they are who they are.

The Hard Truth About Authenticity

Here's the truth you need to hear: **Being authentic is tough.** It means showing up when you don't feel like it. It means doing what's right even when it's inconvenient. It means saying no to things that don't align with your values, even when everyone else is saying yes. It means telling the truth—even when the truth is uncomfortable. **It means walking the talk.** And yes, it will challenge you.

But this is where the real power lies. When you start living authentically, you **gain respect**—not just from others, but from yourself. You'll look in the mirror and know you're the real deal. You won't have to lie to yourself about who you are or what you stand for.

The guru doesn't **negotiate** with their integrity. They don't bend their values to fit the situation. They know that **any compromise of integrity is a compromise of the self.**

3. Practices for Living with Integrity in the Modern World

Okay, now you know the stakes. Integrity isn't optional. But how do you integrate it into your life? How do you start living like a guru—authentically and consistently—when the world around you is full of distractions and temptations? I'll tell you how.

Step 1: Define Your Core Values

Before you can live with integrity, you need to **know what you stand for.** What are your non-negotiables? What values do you want to guide your life? These should be clear, and they should be **simple**. Don't overcomplicate this. Think honesty, loyalty, compassion, responsibility—whatever resonates with you at the core.

- **Exercise:** Write down your top three core values. These are your **guiding principles**—your compass for every decision you make. When you face tough choices, ask yourself: **Does this align with my core values?** If it doesn't, don't do it.

Step 2: Practice Radical Honesty

Integrity starts with honesty—and that means **radical honesty**. No more hiding behind excuses, half-truths, or sugarcoating reality. The guru speaks the truth, even when it's uncomfortable. But it's not just about telling others the truth—it's about telling **yourself** the truth, too.

- **Exercise:** Practice radical honesty for the next week. In your conversations, in your self-reflection—be blunt with yourself. If something's not working, own it. If you're being lazy, admit it. If you're hiding your true feelings, face them head-on.

Step 3: Align Your Actions with Your Words

This is where most people fail. They say one thing and do another. **You have to align what you say with what you do.** No more empty promises. If you say you'll show up, you show up. If you say you'll do something, you do it—**no matter what.**

- **Exercise:** Commit to one action this week that reinforces your integrity. It could be something small, like calling someone you owe an apology to, or following through on a commitment you've been avoiding. But follow through—no excuses.

4. The Final Word on Integrity: No Compromise

Listen, integrity isn't negotiable. **If you lose your integrity, you lose yourself.** You can't fake it. You can't pretend to be something you're not. The guru doesn't negotiate with integrity—they live it. And if you want to walk that path, if you want to live authentically and consistently, you've got to be willing to **face yourself** every day.

No more excuses. No more pretending. No more cutting corners. **Your life, your success, and your spiritual growth depend on this.**

So, **stop talking about it**. Stop reading about it. **Live it.** You have the power to create the integrity-filled life you want, but you've got to start now. And when you do, the world won't just notice—it'll reflect your truth back to you in ways you can't even imagine.

Get to work.

Part 4: Practical Wisdom for Everyday Life

You want the secret to living a powerful, fulfilling life? It's not about seeking more knowledge. It's not about reading a hundred more self-help books. **It's about applying what you already know.** This is where the rubber meets the road. If you want to embody the wisdom of a guru, you've got to bring that wisdom down from the clouds and make it real. Real life. Real relationships. Real decisions. **You've got to live it.**

A guru doesn't just spout wisdom and then go off to meditate in a cave. They **live** the wisdom in the middle of the mess. They know that spirituality isn't something to compartmentalize—it's something to **infuse into everything.** Every decision, every relationship, every action. **Spiritual wisdom is practical. It's not just theory.**

And don't kid yourself. You've got choices to make. You've got decisions to make every single day that demand your spiritual wisdom. Relationships to manage. Work to do. Conflicts to resolve. And those choices matter—because, **ultimately, your life is a reflection of how well you apply your spiritual wisdom to the real world.**

If you want to live like a guru, it's time to stop talking about spirituality and **start practicing it.** Every. Single. Day.

1. Applying Spiritual Wisdom to Daily Decisions

Listen up—**life is full of decisions.** Some small, some big. But what separates a guru from the rest of the pack is how they make those decisions. A guru doesn't get caught up in the drama. They don't make decisions based on emotion, impulse, or external pressure. They make decisions grounded in spiritual clarity, rooted in **wisdom.**

So, how do you make decisions like a guru? Simple. You check in with **what really matters.** What are your values? What is your highest intention? Too often, we make decisions based on fear, ego, or instant gratification. The guru knows that the only thing that will create lasting fulfillment is choosing in alignment with the **truth** of who you are.

Here's the kicker: You don't have to go sit in a lotus pose for hours to connect to your truth. The truth is always available to you. **You access it through awareness.** When a decision arises, take a moment—just a moment—and ask yourself: *"What's my highest truth in this situation? What would I do if I were grounded in integrity and wisdom?"*

Example: You're offered a new job, but something feels off about it. Your ego says, "Go for it. It's a step up. It's more money." But your gut knows something isn't right. A guru listens to that gut. The guru doesn't make decisions based on external validation or ego-driven desires. They tune in to their higher self and make the choice that aligns with their **authentic values**, even if it means saying no to the apparent opportunity.

2. Navigating Relationships with Spiritual Wisdom

Let's get real—relationships are messy. But guess what? That's where you'll find out if you really have spiritual wisdom or if you're just spitting out lines from some book. **The real test of your spiritual growth is how you show up in your relationships.** Not how much you can meditate or chant, but how you act when your partner pushes your buttons, when your boss takes credit for your work, or when your friend is in crisis.

A guru doesn't walk around in a spiritual bubble, detached from the world. A guru lives with compassion and wisdom in every interaction, no matter how small or messy. The guru doesn't react—they **respond.**

The key is this: **You have a choice in every moment.** You can react with anger, defensiveness, or pride. Or you can choose to act from a place of wisdom, love, and understanding. The guru doesn't try to control others. They know they can only control themselves. And that means cultivating the **ability to stay grounded** in the face of conflict.

- **Example:** Your partner snaps at you. You could snap back. Or you could take a breath, recognize that this reaction isn't about you, and respond with compassion. Maybe your partner's having a bad day. Maybe they're frustrated and you're the closest target. A guru listens, doesn't take things personally, and doesn't escalate the situation. Instead, they remain calm and seek understanding.

This doesn't mean being a doormat. It means being strong in **your own wisdom.** When you come from a place of compassion and clarity, you elevate the entire relationship. You raise the vibration of the interaction and the situation changes. **This is how the guru moves through the world.**

3. Living in Alignment with Your Spiritual Path

This is where the rubber really hits the road. **Spirituality is not something you pick up when you feel like it.** It's something you live **every single day.** You don't just go to church, meditate, or read a book and then go back to living like everyone else. You live your spiritual principles all the time—no exceptions.

Every action you take is either in alignment with your spiritual path, or it's not. **This is the bottom line.** And you can't fake it. If you're saying one thing and doing another, you're out of alignment. Simple as that. When your actions, thoughts, and intentions are aligned with your values and spiritual beliefs, you feel a sense of peace, fulfillment, and **clarity.**

A guru isn't someone who lives one way in the public eye and another in private. A guru **embodies** their spiritual wisdom in all situations. When you walk the talk, you **integrate your spiritual path into your daily life.**

Example: You're juggling work, family, and personal commitments. You're stressed and overwhelmed, and it's easy to justify cutting corners—telling a white lie here, skipping a task there. But you know what? **The guru doesn't make excuses.** They don't cut corners because they know that every small compromise is a step away from who they truly are. They stay in integrity, even when it's inconvenient.

4. Exercises to Embody Spiritual Wisdom in the Real World

Alright, now you've got the theory. But it's time to **do the work**. I'm not here to just talk about spiritual wisdom—I'm here to show you how to embody it in the real world. Here are some practices you can start using today to bring your wisdom into every corner of your life.

Exercise 1: Decision-Making with Clarity

Every time you face a decision today, ask yourself: "What would my higher self choose in this situation?" Before making any decision—big or small—take a moment to check in with your **deepest truth**. This simple practice will help you stop making decisions from ego or impulse. It will train you to align your actions with your higher purpose.

Exercise 2: Compassionate Communication

The next time you're in a conversation where conflict arises or someone pushes your buttons, pause. Take a breath. Instead of reacting, try this: **Respond with compassion and curiosity.** Ask yourself, "What's really going on here?" By responding from a place of understanding, you shift the energy of the conversation and avoid unnecessary conflict. You'll be amazed at how often this approach changes the entire dynamic.

Exercise 3: Alignment Check

At the end of each day, ask yourself: "Did my actions today align with my values?" Be brutally honest. Did you act in integrity? Were you kind when you could have been impatient? Were you present with others? Were you grounded in your spiritual path? This practice helps you **course-correct** if you've gotten off track, and it solidifies the habit of living with authenticity.

5. *The Final Word: Live It or Quit Talking About It*

Enough talk. **Spiritual wisdom is not about theory.** It's not about what you know. It's about what you **do**. So stop reading and start living. Apply this wisdom in your relationships. Apply it in your decisions. Apply it in your daily actions. **Live like the guru you are.**

When you stop talking and start doing, the world will change. You'll change. And when that happens, everything else will follow.

Chapter 9: Embracing Challenges: The Guru's Resilience and Strength

Part 1: Reframing Challenges

———

Let's get one thing straight: **Life is full of challenges.** If you're waiting for the moment when everything clicks and you can sit back and relax, you're wasting time. The truth is, challenges aren't some unfortunate byproduct of life; they are **life**. The question isn't whether you'll face challenges—it's how you will *respond* when they come knocking at your door.

And guess what? **A guru doesn't view challenges as obstacles.** No. They see them as opportunities. Opportunities for growth, for clarity, for strength. The guru understands that growth is never linear—it's messy, it's hard, and it's full of bumps and bruises. But here's the secret: *Without those challenges, you don't grow*. Period.

So, stop complaining about your problems. **You've got them, fine**—we all do. Now, what are you going to do about it? The guru doesn't waste time feeling sorry for themselves. They're too busy looking for the lesson, the growth, and the strength that can be forged in the fire of adversity.

If you want to walk this path like a guru, you've got to **shift your perspective**. You've got to stop seeing challenges as something to avoid and start embracing them as part of your evolution.

1. The Guru's View of Obstacles: Opportunities in Disguise

Listen up, because this is important: **Every challenge you face is an opportunity for you to grow.** Every hardship, every struggle, is a chance to level up. You want to be stronger, smarter, and more resilient? Then you need to learn how to see challenges for what they are: opportunities in disguise.

Take a moment. Think of the toughest times in your life. The times when you were knocked down, when you wanted to quit. Now, look at where you are now. **Aren't you stronger for having gone through that?** Maybe it didn't feel like it at the time. But here's the truth: you learned something. You grew. You discovered something about yourself you didn't know before.

The guru gets this. They know that **the real work happens when life gets uncomfortable**. It's easy to meditate when everything's smooth. It's easy to talk about love and compassion when you're not being tested. But the true measure of your growth happens when life gets real, when you're facing down a challenge and you still choose to show up with integrity, clarity, and resilience.

Here's how you can start reframing challenges today: Instead of focusing on the "problem" you're facing, focus on **what you can learn** from it. Ask yourself: *What is this teaching me? How can I become a better version of myself through this struggle?* The moment you stop viewing the challenge as something to fear and start seeing it as an opportunity to grow, you shift your entire relationship with adversity.

2. *Shifting From Problem-Solving to Embracing the Journey*

Now, this might sound a little counterintuitive at first, but hear me out: **Stop trying to "solve" your problems**. That's right. Instead of focusing on how to fix everything, focus on how to grow through it.

A lot of people approach challenges with a mindset of "How can I fix this? How can I make this go away?" But the guru knows the secret: **You don't need to fix everything.** Sometimes, the best thing you can do is lean in and allow the experience to shape you. Growth isn't about eliminating pain; it's about learning how to move through it with grace and strength.

Take this example: Think about a time you went through something really tough—maybe you lost a job, maybe you were betrayed by a close friend, maybe you hit a financial crisis. What was your first reaction? Likely, you tried to find a quick fix. You wanted to jump out of the discomfort and make it better, right?

But here's the kicker: **The discomfort is part of the process.** The struggle, the pain, the uncertainty—they're all part of the journey. And if you keep looking for an escape, you'll miss the lessons hidden in that struggle. The guru understands this. They're not trying to escape discomfort—they're learning to navigate it, to use it to propel themselves forward.

This doesn't mean being passive. It means **being present**. It means looking at the situation not as something to "fix" but as an experience that can teach you something. Instead of just searching for the solution, ask yourself: *What is this challenge here to teach me?*

3. *The Power of Perspective: How to Reframe Your Challenges*

You've got a choice, always. When faced with a challenge, you can either get caught up in the drama or you can take a step back and **reframe the situation**. The guru knows that the key to resilience is reframing the challenge in a way that empowers them. They don't let external circumstances dictate their internal state.

Here's how you do it:

- **Identify the story you're telling yourself.** When things go wrong, what's the first thing that pops into your mind? Do you tell yourself: *"This isn't fair. I don't deserve this. This is too much"*? If so, you're falling into the victim mindset. Stop. That's not going to serve you. Instead, reframe it. Ask yourself: *"What can I learn from this situation? What's the opportunity here?"*
- **Focus on what you can control.** The guru doesn't waste energy on what's outside their control. Instead, they focus on their response. No matter what's going on around you, **you can control your reaction.** You can choose how to show up. You can choose to respond with resilience, strength, and clarity. You don't need to control everything to be in control of your life.
- **Get comfortable with uncertainty.** We're all conditioned to want security. We want certainty. But guess what? The guru knows that

life is unpredictable. The more you try to control everything, the more stressed you'll be. The real power comes from learning to live **with uncertainty**. When you stop fearing the unknown and instead embrace it as a natural part of life, you stop letting challenges throw you off course.

4. Practical Exercise: Reframe Your Current Challenges

Alright, now it's time to get to work. Here's an exercise to start shifting your mindset from "problem-solving" to embracing challenges as part of your growth process.

1. **Write down the biggest challenge you're currently facing.** This could be anything—a difficult relationship, a financial issue, work stress, health problems, etc. Write it out in detail.
2. **Identify the negative story you're telling yourself about it.** What's your default narrative? Are you seeing this as a setback? A sign that something's wrong? Write that down.
3. **Reframe the situation.** Now, flip the script. Instead of seeing the challenge as an obstacle, ask yourself: *What's the lesson here? What can I learn from this experience?* Maybe it's a lesson in patience. Maybe it's showing you where you need to be more assertive. Maybe it's teaching you how to trust the process.
4. **Commit to an empowered action.** What's one thing you can do to move forward in this situation, even if it's just a small step? Take action. The key to reframing challenges is **action**. Don't just think about it—do something that aligns with your new perspective.

5. Final Word: The Guru's Resilience Is Your Resilience

The guru doesn't back down from challenges. They don't wish them away. They embrace them. Because they know, deep down, that their growth depends on it. They've mastered the art of reframing difficulties and turning them into stepping stones on the path to higher consciousness.

So, stop seeing challenges as obstacles. They're not. They're the very thing that will elevate you to the next level. Embrace them, learn from them, and keep moving forward. Because the more you do, the more **unstoppable** you become.

The journey is the destination. So get comfortable with it. Embrace it. And rise to the occasion.

Part 2: Building Inner Resilience

———

You want to be a guru? Then stop waiting for life to hand you a smooth ride. **Resilience is the game, and challenges are your training ground.** You want mental toughness? You want emotional grit? Good. You're in the right place. But let me warn you: **this isn't for the weak.** This is for those who are ready to step up, face the heat, and push through the grind.

When a guru faces adversity, they don't crumble. They don't play the victim. They don't throw their hands in the air and scream, "Why me?" No, they get to work. They know that **resilience isn't something you're born with—it's something you build**. It's earned, forged in the fire of struggle, and strengthened with every decision to keep going, no matter how hard it gets.

So, if you're serious about building your inner strength, you need to be ready to do the work. Let's break it down. We'll talk about mental toughness, emotional resilience, and how you can develop these critical skills through mindfulness, self-compassion, and grit.

1. The Guru's Mental Toughness: It's About Staying in the Game

Mental toughness isn't about being unshakable. It's not about pretending you don't feel fear or doubt. No, **mental toughness is about pushing through despite fear and doubt.** It's about showing up, day in and day out, regardless of what's going on inside your head. **It's about doing what needs to be done, even when your mind tells you to quit.**

A guru isn't invincible. They get tired, frustrated, and stressed like the rest of us. But here's where they differ from the average person: **they know how to keep their focus.** When everything around them is falling apart, the guru keeps their head in the game. They stay present. They don't get swept away by the noise of their thoughts. Instead, they focus on what needs to be done, one step at a time.

Let's get real for a moment. We've all been there. Life hits hard, and suddenly we're overwhelmed. Our minds race with a thousand thoughts: *"I can't do this. This is too much. I'm not good enough. This isn't fair."* And when those thoughts flood in, they have the power to stop us dead in our tracks.

But a guru doesn't let those thoughts control their actions. They **acknowledge the thoughts**—they don't ignore them—but they don't let them dictate their behavior. They recognize the thought as just that: a thought. It's not the truth. It's just a fleeting moment in their mind. So, they dismiss it and stay focused on the task at hand.

How can you develop this mental toughness?

- **Practice staying present.** When you feel that mental chatter ramping up, bring your attention back to the here and now. Breathe. Focus on the next step, the next decision. It's all about staying in the moment.
- **Challenge negative thoughts.** When your mind tells you that you can't, flip it. Ask yourself: *"What's the evidence that I can't? What's the proof that I can?"*
- **Push through discomfort.** Stop avoiding the hard things. If you want to develop mental toughness, you have to embrace discomfort. Whether it's a tough conversation, a difficult project, or an uncomfortable emotion, don't run from it. Face it head-on.

2. Emotional Resilience: Bouncing Back From Life's Hits

Here's the truth: **you're going to get knocked down.** That's just part of the deal. **What matters is how quickly you get back up.**

Emotional resilience is the ability to bounce back from setbacks without letting them define you. It's about not getting stuck in the emotional drama when things go wrong. And I'm not talking about bottling up your emotions. **Emotional resilience doesn't mean ignoring your pain.** It means feeling it, acknowledging it, and then letting it go so that it doesn't hold you back.

The guru knows that emotions are fleeting. They're not something to avoid—they're something to process. When life hits hard, the guru doesn't suppress their anger, sadness, or frustration. They feel it. **They sit with it.** They allow it to pass through them, not linger. And when it's gone, they move on.

If you want to develop emotional resilience, you have to stop identifying with your emotions. You are **not** your emotions. You experience them, but they don't control you. A guru understands that their emotional state doesn't dictate their worth. They don't let a bad day, a tough conversation, or an uncomfortable situation determine how they feel about themselves.

How to build emotional resilience?

- **Practice mindfulness.** Mindfulness isn't just about calming your mind. It's about noticing your emotions without getting caught up in them. When you're angry or upset, acknowledge it. Don't push it away. Sit with it. Let it be there. Then choose to let it go when it's time.
- **Develop self-compassion.** Don't beat yourself up when you fail or make mistakes. Recognize that you're human. Offer yourself the same kindness and understanding you'd give a friend who's struggling. **Treat yourself like you matter.**
- **Create a support system.** Emotional resilience is not about being strong all the time. It's about knowing when to lean on others. Don't isolate yourself. Surround yourself with people who uplift and support you, especially when life gets tough.

3. Grit: The Unshakable Determination to Keep Going

If there's one quality that sets the guru apart from the average person, it's **grit**. Grit is that unwavering determination to keep going, no matter what. It's not about being the smartest or the most talented. It's about being willing to work when it's hard, to stay committed when everyone else is giving up.

The guru knows that success is never instant. It takes time. It takes effort. It takes **relentless persistence**. You don't just wake up one day with everything figured out. You get up, you work, and you keep working, no matter how long it takes.

Building grit isn't about *hoping* things get easier. It's about **embracing the challenge and pushing through anyway**. It's about showing up for yourself when no one else is looking, even when it feels like you're getting nowhere.

How do you develop grit?

- **Commit to the long-term vision.** Grit is about seeing the bigger picture. It's about knowing that the struggle is temporary, but the growth is permanent. **Keep your eyes on the prize**, even when the path is unclear.
- **Set small, achievable goals.** Grit doesn't mean charging forward without strategy. It means breaking your big vision down into manageable steps. Celebrate the small wins along the way to keep your momentum going.
- **Embrace failure as part of the process.** Failure isn't the end; it's just another step in the journey. When you fail, you don't quit. You learn, you adjust, and you try again. **Fail forward.** Every setback is a setup for a comeback.

4. Practical Exercise: Building Your Resilience Toolkit

Now, let's get practical. Here's an exercise to build your inner resilience. Follow these steps every day, and watch yourself grow stronger.

1. **Identify a current challenge.** Pick something in your life that's testing your resilience right now. It could be a work situation, a relationship issue, or a personal goal you're struggling with.
2. **Observe your emotions.** Take five minutes to sit quietly and observe the emotions that arise when you think about this challenge. What feelings are coming up? **Don't judge them—just**

notice them.

3. **Reframe the challenge.** Now, step back and reframe the situation. Instead of seeing it as something that's happening *to* you, ask: *What can I learn from this? How can I use this challenge to grow stronger?*

4. **Set a small action step.** What's one thing you can do today to move through this challenge? It doesn't have to be big. Just pick one small action step to show up for yourself.

5. **Practice self-compassion.** At the end of the day, reflect on how you handled the situation. Acknowledge your effort, even if things didn't go perfectly. Treat yourself with kindness and remember: you're in the process of building resilience, not perfection.

The Strength You Build Is Your Power

Resilience isn't a trait you're born with. It's a skill you develop through consistent effort. The guru knows this. They don't shy away from challenges. They welcome them. They understand that **the more you embrace adversity, the stronger you become**. So get up, get moving, and get tough. Life is waiting for you to show up.

Part 3: The Role of Suffering in Transformation

Alright, listen up. Suffering isn't something to fear. It's not something to avoid. It's not some curse that happens to you because the universe has it out for you. **Suffering is your ticket to growth.** And if you're serious about becoming a modern-day guru, you need to get that into your head right now.

You've been sold a lie that life should be smooth, easy, and free of pain. That's a fairy tale. The truth? Life is tough. It throws curveballs. People betray you. Things don't go your way. You fail, you get hurt, and you question everything. **That's life.**

But what do you do with it? The gurus know. **They turn suffering into their greatest teacher.** They don't run from it. They don't whine about it. They don't look for someone to blame. **They use suffering to evolve.**

It's time to stop seeing challenges as roadblocks and start seeing them as invitations. **Invitations to wake up. Invitations to expand. Invitations to discover just how deep your strength really goes.** Because when you face suffering head-on, without flinching, you discover something remarkable about yourself. You become more, not less. But only if you have the courage to embrace it.

1. The Guru's Approach to Suffering: It's Not What Happens to You, It's What You Do With It

Here's the thing about gurus: they don't sugarcoat suffering. They don't pretend it's not happening. They don't wear rose-colored glasses and say, "Oh, it's all part of the plan." **They get real with it.**

A true guru understands that suffering is a necessary part of the human experience. They know that **pain is not just inevitable; it's essential**. It's like a forge—where metal is heated until it becomes malleable. It's under extreme heat and pressure that the most beautiful, resilient things are created. **And so are you.**

But you have to choose. You can either let suffering break you, or you can **use it to sharpen yourself.** The guru never sees suffering as a final destination. They see it as a crossroads: one path leads to victimhood and bitterness; the other leads to wisdom and strength. The choice is yours.

Think about this: how many times has a challenge in your life caused you to question everything? Maybe it was a breakup, the loss of a job, or the death of someone close to you. The pain is real, no doubt about it. But I'm telling you—**this pain has a purpose.**

Take a minute and think about a tough time in your life, something that felt like it would break you. When you look back, do you see how that moment pushed you to grow? Maybe it taught you resilience, humility, or the value of perseverance. Maybe it gave you a deeper understanding of what truly matters.

This is what the guru knows. They use suffering as a stepping stone to something greater. They don't resist it. They don't run away from it. They lean into it and ask, "What is this teaching me?"

2. Seeing Difficulty as an Invitation for Deeper Learning

You want to grow spiritually, right? You want to elevate your thinking and your life? Then stop thinking of suffering as a problem that needs fixing. **It's not a problem; it's a teacher.**

The guru views every difficulty as a chance to learn something deeper about themselves and the world. **They see challenges as opportunities to expand their consciousness.** It's a shift in mindset, and it's one of the most powerful lessons you can learn.

Let me give you an example: Have you ever had a tough relationship, one where it felt like everything was falling apart? The guru doesn't see that as a failure. **They see it as an invitation to understand love on a deeper**

level. Maybe they learn about their own boundaries, their own needs, or their own fears. The difficulty pushes them to explore deeper aspects of themselves—parts they may have never noticed before.

The guru doesn't just survive suffering. They **transform** through it. Every hardship is a chance to go deeper. A chance to strip away the superficial and get to the heart of who they are.

Here's a question for you: **What suffering in your life could be calling you to expand your consciousness?** What lessons are hidden in the struggle you're facing right now? Don't just complain about the pain. Look at it square in the eyes and ask, *What is this trying to teach me?*

3. Building Self-Awareness Through Struggle

Self-awareness isn't something that's handed to you on a silver platter. It's something you earn, and you earn it through the toughest experiences in your life. When you're going through hard times, that's when you **really get to know yourself.** That's when your character is tested. That's when you find out if you have the grit, the patience, and the perseverance to rise up.

The guru uses suffering to increase self-awareness. **When life goes sideways, they don't point fingers.** They don't blame others. Instead, they ask, *"What's going on inside me? What part of me is reacting this way? Why does this situation trigger me?"*

This is the key to unlocking personal and spiritual growth: understanding **your own reactions.** When something difficult happens, how do you respond? Do you lash out? Do you shut down? Do you look for someone to rescue you? Or do you stand your ground and say, *"This is a challenge. What can I learn from it?"*

Your reaction is your power. It's your opportunity to practice self-control, patience, and emotional intelligence. So when life knocks you down, don't just get angry or frustrated. **Pause. Reflect.** Ask yourself: *What am I really feeling? Why am I feeling this way?*

The guru knows that self-awareness isn't about avoiding pain; it's about understanding it. It's about feeling the pain, but not being consumed by it. It's about **using that pain to dig deeper into your own psyche** and find out who you really are beneath all the layers.

4. Practical Steps to Turn Suffering Into Transformation

Here's how you can start using suffering as a catalyst for growth. This isn't about becoming numb to pain. It's about transforming your relationship with it.

- **Step 1: Stop Running From Pain**
  The first step is to stop pretending that pain doesn't exist. The world doesn't owe you a perfect life. Accept that suffering is part of the deal. When you face a challenge, don't run from it. Sit with it. Be with it. Look it in the face. **Feel it.**
- **Step 2: Ask the Right Questions**
  When you face adversity, ask yourself, *What's this teaching me? What's inside me that this situation is trying to reveal?* The right questions unlock the door to deeper wisdom. Don't waste your energy on self-pity or blame. Use the energy to learn.
- **Step 3: Find the Lesson in Every Difficulty**
  Every challenge holds a lesson. Whether it's learning about your own limits, your patience, or your capacity for love, there's something there for you to uncover. Don't just survive it—**embrace it as an opportunity for growth.**
- **Step 4: Practice Gratitude**
  This one sounds counterintuitive, but it works. **Gratitude in the face of suffering shifts your mindset.** Instead of focusing on what's wrong, focus on what's right. Find something to be grateful for, even in the most difficult situations. You'll be surprised at how much strength that brings.
- **Step 5: Let It Change You**
  The final step is to **allow the suffering to change you.** Every

hardship, every challenge, every difficult moment should leave you different. If you aren't evolving through suffering, then you're resisting the process. Allow your struggles to refine you, to make you wiser, more compassionate, and more grounded.

Suffering is the Path to Mastery

You want to master your life? Then embrace suffering. Stop seeing it as a punishment or a burden. See it as a **tool for transformation**. You can't go around it. You can't hide from it. But you can use it to sharpen your spirit and build your strength.

The guru understands this better than anyone. They know that the road to enlightenment is paved with pain, struggle, and discomfort. But they also know that **the deeper you go into your suffering, the more you grow**. So face it. Embrace it. Let it change you. And watch as you become the person you were always meant to be.

Part 4: Tools for Resilience

———

Let's cut to the chase: Life isn't a smooth ride. It's messy. It's hard. And sometimes, you're gonna feel like you're getting the crap kicked out of you. **Welcome to reality.** The question is, what are you gonna do about it? How are you gonna handle the heat when it comes at you from all sides? Are you gonna crumble? Or are you gonna stand tall, face the storm, and come out the other side stronger?

The gurus didn't get to where they are by pretending life was all sunshine and rainbows. No. They built **mental toughness, emotional resilience, and unshakable strength** through practice. They used tools—practical, effective tools—to bounce back from life's toughest blows. You can too.

But it's not enough to talk about resilience. You have to **train** for it. **Resilience is a skill**, just like any other. And like any skill, it requires repetition, discipline, and the willingness to keep going when it gets hard.

In this chapter, I'm going to give you the tools to build your resilience. You want to become unbreakable, unstoppable? These exercises are for you.

1. Affirmations: Rewiring Your Mindset

Let me be blunt: if you think that everything's going to be sunshine just by thinking happy thoughts, you're fooling yourself. But here's the thing: **your mind is powerful**. You've heard it before, but now it's time to make it real. What you **think** shapes what you experience. So, if you constantly think, "I'm a failure" or "I can't handle this," guess what? Your brain will find all the evidence to prove it.

Affirmations are a tool that the guru uses to shift their mindset from victimhood to power. They use words, words that carry energy and strength, to change their reality. Don't just sit there waiting for things to change by magic. **Speak your strength into existence.** You've got to counteract all that negative thinking with positive affirmations that hit hard.

How to do it:

1. **Write down a few core affirmations** that align with your goal of building resilience. Keep them short and powerful.
    - "I am stronger than my challenges."
    - "I grow through every difficulty."
    - "Every setback is a setup for my comeback."
    - "I am unshakable in the face of adversity."
2. **Repeat them daily.** Say them out loud, stand in front of a mirror if you have to. You need to hear yourself say it. Internalize it. Say it until it becomes as natural as breathing.
3. **Visualize** yourself embodying these words. Picture yourself handling life's hardest blows with calm, composure, and strength. If you need proof this works, look no further than professional athletes and high-performers. They do it all the time. If it's good enough for them, it's good enough for you.

2. Visualization: Training Your Mind for Success

Here's the deal: your mind doesn't know the difference between what's real and what you vividly imagine. **That's how powerful visualization is.** When you picture yourself succeeding, overcoming obstacles, or responding to stress in a calm and composed way, your mind treats it as real. You're wiring yourself for success. You're training for your future, now.

The gurus know this. That's why they spend time visualizing their responses to challenges. They know the obstacles are coming—they don't wish they'll disappear. Instead, they **prepare for them.** They rehearse their victories in their minds before they're ever tested.

How to do it:

1. **Get clear on the challenge you want to overcome**—whether it's a

big work deadline, a personal conflict, or dealing with an emotional trigger.

2. **Visualize yourself handling the challenge with complete calm and resilience.**
     - See yourself responding with clarity, confidence, and poise.
     - Picture yourself bouncing back from setbacks.
     - Imagine the emotions you would feel in the moment—strength, confidence, and control.
3. **Do this every morning or before difficult situations.** Your mind needs repetition. The more you see yourself handling pressure with ease, the more likely you are to do it in real life.

By visualizing yourself **succeeding** instead of stressing over failure, you condition your mind to respond with power. You make resilience your default setting.

3. Positive Reframing: Turning Obstacles Into Opportunities

Life is full of obstacles. Get used to it. The difference between people who thrive and people who falter? **Perspective.** People who succeed know that every obstacle is just a lesson in disguise. The moment you shift your mindset from "This is terrible" to "What can I learn from this?" you put yourself in a position of power. You stop being the victim and become the victor.

You need to **reframe** every negative experience. This is a practice that the guru masters over time. They understand that **life isn't happening to them; it's happening for them.** Even the most challenging experiences can serve as fuel for growth.

How to do it:

1. **Catch yourself when you're in a negative spiral.** The moment you start thinking, "I can't do this," or "This is just too much," STOP.
2. **Ask yourself, "What's the lesson here?"**
     - Instead of thinking, "I'm never going to make it," try,

> "What can I learn from this situation that will make me stronger?"
> - ○ Instead of thinking, "This is unfair," ask, "How can I turn this to my advantage?"
> - ○ Instead of stressing over a setback, think, "This is a chance to grow and adapt."

3. **Make it a habit** to reframe every challenge, every setback, every failure. The more you practice it, the more natural it becomes. Soon, you'll find yourself seeing every obstacle as a stepping stone to growth.

Reframing doesn't mean ignoring the pain or pretending everything is fine. It means **choosing how to respond** to the pain. And by responding with strength, curiosity, and resilience, you make sure that pain doesn't control you.

4. Building Grit: Sticking It Out When the Going Gets Tough

You want resilience? You need grit. And grit isn't something you're born with. **It's something you build.** It's the ability to keep going when everyone else gives up. It's pushing through discomfort, doubt, and fear to achieve your goal, no matter what. The guru doesn't back down in the face of adversity. They meet it with determination.

You want to develop resilience? Then develop grit. Period.

How to do it:

1. **Commit to your goals.** This isn't about half-assed effort. If you want resilience, you need to commit to something bigger than your current pain. No excuses. No retreat. If you're in, you're in.
2. **Take consistent action.** Every single day, take at least one step toward your goal. Whether it's a small task or a major hurdle, make sure you're moving forward.
3. **When it gets tough, don't stop.** Push through the discomfort. The guru doesn't quit when things get hard—they double down.

The harder it gets, the more they push forward. Because they know that the prize is on the other side of pain.

4. **Embrace failure as part of the process.** If you fail, so what? Failing is part of the game. Every failure teaches you something. The guru knows that failure is just feedback. Learn from it, get up, and keep going.

5. Daily Resilience Practice: Strengthening Your Emotional Muscles

Just like physical fitness, emotional resilience needs **consistent training**. You can't expect to be strong if you only work on your resilience when things are tough. You need to **build the muscles** of resilience every single day.

How to do it:

1. **Set aside 10-15 minutes each day for resilience training.** It could be affirmations, visualization, journaling, or even a short meditation on resilience. Make it a ritual.
2. **Track your progress.** Each week, reflect on how you handled challenges. Celebrate your wins. Learn from your losses. This helps you see just how much you've grown.
3. **Commit to daily practice.** Make resilience as much a part of your routine as brushing your teeth. When you train your mind and emotions daily, you become unshakable.

Resilience Isn't a Trait, It's a Practice

The difference between those who survive and those who thrive is resilience. You can talk about being strong all day long, but **true strength is built through practice.** You want to be a guru in the making? You want to handle life's toughest challenges with the composure and power of a seasoned master?

Then start practicing now. Use these tools. Build your resilience. And when life throws its next curveball, you'll be ready. You won't just handle it—you'll **rise from it** stronger than ever.

Chapter 10: Living the Guru Mindset: A Path to Mastery and Legacy

Part 1: Mastery Over the Self

Let's get this straight right now: **If you want to be a true master in life, you've got to start with mastering yourself.** Forget the fancy philosophies, the meditation retreats, or the latest self-help guru with their five-step programs. At the end of the day, it's about you—your thoughts, your emotions, your actions. **Master yourself, and everything else falls into place.**

The gurus didn't get where they are by waiting for someone else to change the game for them. They didn't sit around hoping for the perfect circumstances or waiting for someone else to save them. They took ownership. They took responsibility. They **mastered themselves**.

And here's the thing: mastery over yourself is not a one-time event. It's not some certificate you hang on your wall. It's a **continuous process**. Every day. Every hour. Every decision. You either control your mind, or it controls you. You either master your emotions, or they run wild, dragging you around like a dog on a leash. You either take command of your actions, or you stay stuck in the same old patterns.

This is the path the guru walks, and it's the path you've got to walk if you want to move forward. It's the hard road—the road of constant self-discipline, rigorous honesty, and unflinching commitment to becoming your best.

Mastering Your Thoughts: The First Battle

You think the guru is some kind of magical being who's never plagued by doubt or negative thoughts? **Think again.** Every human experiences those moments when the mind races, when doubts creep in, when the inner voice tells you that you're not enough. The difference between you and a guru is this: **they don't let those thoughts control them.**

You can't control every thought that pops into your head. Let me repeat that: You cannot control every thought. But here's the kicker: **You can control how you respond to those thoughts.**

The guru knows this, which is why they've developed the ability to notice their thoughts without getting swept away by them. They observe their thoughts, but they don't attach to them. They don't identify with them. They know that **thoughts are just thoughts**—they're not who you are. They're not your reality unless you allow them to be.

How to master your thoughts:

1. **Awareness:** The first step is to become aware of the thoughts that dominate your mind. Are they negative? Are they self-limiting? Recognize that these thoughts are just passing clouds—they don't define you.
2. **Interrupt the Pattern:** When negative thoughts arise, **interrupt them.** You don't need to fight them, but you can challenge them. Ask yourself, "Is this thought serving me? Is this thought true? What else could I believe instead?"
3. **Replace and Redirect:** Once you've identified a negative thought, replace it with a more empowering one. Every time you catch yourself thinking something limiting, immediately **reframe** it. "I'm not good enough" becomes "I am growing, and I'm learning."
4. **Consistent Practice:** This is not a one-time deal. You've got to make it a habit to monitor your thoughts throughout the day. Eventually, you won't even need to make the conscious effort—it will be automatic.

The key is **mindfulness.** You'll hear this word a lot because it's the foundation of mental mastery. When you're mindful, you notice the thought before it spirals into something bigger. And the moment you notice it, you regain control.

Mastering Your Emotions: Don't Let Them Run the Show

Let's be real: emotions are like wild animals. They can be powerful, unpredictable, and downright dangerous if you don't know how to tame them. The gurus didn't become sages by letting their emotions run wild every time they felt anger, frustration, or fear. They **learned how to manage their emotions** instead of being enslaved by them.

When you're reactive, when you let emotions control your decisions, you're on autopilot. You're just reacting to the external world instead of responding with intention. The guru, on the other hand, knows that **emotions are signals, not instructions**. They don't suppress their feelings—they just don't let those feelings dictate their behavior.

How to master your emotions:

1. **Observe First:** Just like with your thoughts, the first step in emotional mastery is **awareness**. When you feel an emotion rising, observe it. Where do you feel it in your body? What triggered it? Take a moment to pause before you react.
2. **Don't React Immediately:** Emotions often push us to react in the heat of the moment. But the guru knows that **reaction is weakness**. Responding is strength. Take a step back, breathe, and give yourself time to assess the situation before reacting.
3. **Ask Yourself: "What Do I Need Right Now?"** Instead of letting your emotions dictate your behavior, ask yourself what you really need in the moment. Do you need a breath? Do you need a break? Do you need to talk to someone?
4. **Practice Self-Compassion:** This one's huge. The guru doesn't beat themselves up for having emotions. They recognize them and **show themselves compassion**. Acknowledge that it's normal to feel upset, angry, or sad—and allow yourself the space to process it.

Remember, emotions are like waves. They'll come and go. If you learn to surf them instead of drown in them, you'll be in control. The guru doesn't try to shut off their emotions; they just don't let them hijack their entire life.

Mastering Your Actions: Aligning with Your Highest Self

Okay, let's talk about the big one: **your actions**. It doesn't matter how well you've mastered your thoughts and emotions if your actions are inconsistent with your highest values. The guru doesn't just talk the talk—they walk the walk. Every action they take is intentional, and every decision they make is aligned with their purpose.

The guru isn't perfect. They mess up. They fall short. But they don't let those mistakes define them. They learn from them. And they **take action** to keep improving.

How to master your actions:

1. **Set Clear Intentions:** You cannot move forward if you don't know where you're going. Set clear, intentional goals that align with your values. Whether it's building your career, improving your relationships, or deepening your spiritual practice, **be clear about what you want.**
2. **Take Consistent Action:** The guru doesn't wait for the "right moment" to act—they act now. They show up, day in and day out, with discipline and focus. Consistency is the secret to mastery. Small, daily actions compound over time.
3. **Accountability:** If you're serious about mastering yourself, you've got to hold yourself accountable. No one else will do it for you. Own your choices. When you screw up, admit it. Learn from it. And move forward.
4. **Reflect and Adjust:** Don't just go through the motions. Reflect on your actions regularly. Are they aligned with your goals? Are they getting you closer to the person you want to become? Make adjustments as needed.

Mastery over your actions isn't about perfection—it's about alignment. It's about making sure every choice, no matter how small, moves you closer to the life you want to create.

Ongoing Process: The Never-Ending Journey of Self-Improvement

Let's be clear: **Mastery is a journey, not a destination.** There's no finish line. The moment you think you've "arrived," you've stopped growing. The guru knows this. That's why they are constantly learning, constantly evolving, constantly pushing the boundaries of their own limitations.

Mastering yourself isn't about achieving perfection—it's about **continuing to improve** every single day. It's about building a mindset of **growth**, where every setback is a lesson, every failure is feedback, and every day is an opportunity to show up as a better version of yourself.

You don't become a guru by sitting back and hoping for things to change. You become a guru by taking action, by committing to the practice of self-mastery, and by relentlessly improving yourself over time.

The Path to Mastery Is Yours to Walk

Now it's up to you. **Mastery is not something you achieve. It's something you live.** You want to think like a guru? Start by mastering yourself. Master your thoughts, emotions, and actions. Build your discipline. Build your focus. Build your resilience. And do it every single day.

This isn't some abstract concept. It's your life. Right now. What are you going to do with it?

The path is clear. It's time to walk it.

Part 2: Leaving a Legacy

———

Listen up. **Legacy isn't about what you leave behind in your will.** It's about what you leave behind in the hearts and minds of others. It's not the stuff that gets passed down—it's the lessons. It's the love. It's the way people remember you when you're no longer in the room. And let me tell you something: **you don't need to wait until you're dead to start building your legacy.**

A guru knows this better than anyone. The guru's life is a blueprint, a roadmap for others to follow. Every action they take, every word they speak, every relationship they nurture, is a conscious effort to leave a mark. But here's the deal: **it's not about fame.** It's not about building a monument to your name. If you're thinking about legacy in terms of how many people will remember you or what your tombstone will say, you're missing the point.

A true legacy, the kind the guru is concerned with, is built on **wisdom, compassion, and service.** And that's what I'm going to drill into your skull right now. You can't leave a meaningful legacy unless you're living for something bigger than yourself. **You can't leave a legacy of wisdom if you're not actively learning and teaching.** You can't leave a legacy of compassion if you're not practicing love and empathy every day. And you sure as hell can't leave a legacy of service if you're not giving to others without expecting anything in return.

If you want to make an impact that lasts long after you're gone, it starts right now, with the choices you make today.

The Guru's View on Legacy

Let me break it down for you. The guru doesn't care about accumulating wealth, accolades, or fame. Sure, they might enjoy a good meal, a roof over their head, and the company of friends—but they understand that all of that is temporary. **What matters most is the ripple effect they create.**

The guru sees every interaction as a chance to leave a piece of themselves behind. When they offer wisdom, they're planting a seed in someone's mind. When they show compassion, they're making a soul feel seen and heard. When they serve, they're demonstrating that life is about more than just you—**it's about the collective.**

So, let me ask you this: What are you leaving behind? **What kind of impact are you making in the lives of others?** Because that's the true measure of success. Not how much you've got, but how much you've given. **Not how many followers you have, but how many people you've helped rise.**

The guru doesn't waste time thinking about legacy in the abstract. They don't stress about what others will think of them when they're gone. What they focus on is **how they show up**—how they're using their time, their energy, their gifts, right now. The idea is simple: **live in such a way that your impact is undeniable.**

When a guru speaks, they speak from experience, from the depth of their own journey. They don't give unsolicited advice—they share what they've learned along the way, and they do it with humility. And that's the kind of legacy they leave behind. A legacy of **truth**. A legacy of **experience**. A legacy of **realness**.

Creating a Legacy of Wisdom

Wisdom isn't something you can buy or inherit. It's something you earn—through your experiences, your failures, your struggles, and your triumphs. If you think wisdom is about memorizing some self-help quotes or copying someone else's beliefs, you've got it all wrong. **True wisdom comes from living a full life and learning from it.**

The guru doesn't sit around waiting for wisdom to come to them. They actively seek it. Every failure is an opportunity to learn. Every success is a chance to reflect. The guru builds their legacy by actively **sharing the wisdom they've earned**, passing it down to those who are ready to listen.

But let me tell you something: You can't just sit on your wisdom. It's not meant to stay locked up inside you. **You have to teach it.**

Here's how you create a legacy of wisdom:

1. **Learn Continuously:** Wisdom isn't static. The guru is constantly learning—whether it's from books, from nature, from people, or from their own mistakes. They never stop seeking knowledge. If you're serious about leaving a legacy of wisdom, you've got to make learning a lifelong pursuit.

2. **Teach Others What You've Learned:** Don't hoard your wisdom. **Pass it on.** You can't take it with you, but you can give it away. Start teaching, whether it's through conversations, writing, or mentoring. If you really want your wisdom to last, **teach others how to think for themselves.**

3. **Live Your Wisdom:** Your life should be the living example of what you teach. If you preach kindness but are rude to the waitress, your wisdom means nothing. If you speak of discipline but can't control your own habits, your wisdom has no weight. **Walk your talk.**

When your wisdom touches others, when they apply what you've shared in their own lives, that's when your legacy takes root.

Creating a Legacy of Compassion

Compassion isn't just a feel-good sentiment. It's an active practice. **It's the ability to meet people where they are, to offer kindness without expectation, and to ease suffering without judgment.**

The guru sees people's pain, and they don't look away. They listen without judgment. They give without expecting anything in return. **They serve because it's the right thing to do**, not because it makes them feel good. Compassion is a way of life, not an occasional act.

Here's how you can build a legacy of compassion:

1. **Practice Empathy:** To be compassionate, you first have to

understand others. You need to step into their shoes. **Listen more than you talk**, and when you speak, make sure it's from a place of understanding.

2. **Be Present:** Compassion isn't about what you do—it's about how you show up. When someone needs you, be there. Not just physically, but emotionally and mentally as well. **Be fully present.**

3. **Offer without Expectations:** If you're giving to someone because you expect something in return, that's not compassion. It's a transaction. True compassion requires you to give freely—**no strings attached**.

A legacy of compassion means that when people remember you, they don't just think of your achievements. They think of how you made them feel. **Did you lift them up or bring them down? Did you make them feel valued or invisible?**

Creating a Legacy of Service

The guru doesn't serve because they need approval, or because they're trying to fill some void inside themselves. They serve because it's who they are. Service is the **unshakable foundation** of their existence.

Your legacy of service isn't about grand gestures. It's about the small, everyday acts. The moments when you choose to put someone else's needs before your own. When you choose to give without taking. When you decide that your purpose on this earth is to help others rise.

Here's how to build a legacy of service:

1. **Serve Without Expectation:** The moment you expect something in return, your service becomes selfish. The guru serves without expectation because they know that **true fulfillment comes from giving.**

2. **Live in Service to a Higher Purpose:** When you serve a higher purpose—whether it's humanity, a cause, or your own community—you create a lasting impact. Your legacy becomes a

ripple in the pond of life, affecting generations to come.

3. **Inspire Others to Serve:** A true legacy of service is one that multiplies. When you inspire others to serve, your impact grows exponentially. Don't just give—teach others to give, too.

Your Legacy Starts Now

This is your call to action: Stop waiting for tomorrow. **Start building your legacy today.** Start showing up with wisdom, compassion, and service in every interaction. Don't wait until you're on your deathbed to realize that you've spent your life chasing the wrong things.

The guru leaves behind a legacy because they've lived a life of purpose. A life where their thoughts, their emotions, and their actions were all aligned with the values of wisdom, compassion, and service. **You can do the same.**

So, what kind of legacy do you want to leave? It's time to decide.

Part 3: Becoming the Guru You Seek

———

Let me get straight to the point. You've spent enough time following other people. **It's time to stop seeking guidance from the outside world and start becoming the guide yourself.** You've been reading self-help books, attending seminars, following gurus on Instagram—and that's fine, but **how long are you going to stay a student?** You've learned the lessons. Now, it's time to step up, embody them, and live them out in your own life.

This chapter isn't about glorifying some "guru" persona. It's about realizing that **the qualities you admire in others**—the wisdom, the calm, the presence, the compassion—they're not out of reach. They're in you, and they always have been. You don't need to wait for permission. **You don't need to be "discovered."**

You're already capable of being the kind of guru you seek. It's time to step into it. **Right now.**

Stop Chasing External Gurus

Here's the deal: **You've been told that someone else has the answers to your problems.** You've been convinced that someone has the key to your happiness, your success, your fulfillment. That's the lie.

Every guru you've followed, admired, or put on a pedestal got there because they took what was already inside them and worked it out through action. They didn't wait for a "guru" to come along. **They realized that the only authority worth following is the one that lives inside you.**

You've got everything you need to lead yourself. You just need to stop searching for answers outside of yourself. Stop listening to every new "guru" who promises you enlightenment in 30 days. Stop looking for validation in other people's teachings. The truth is, **you've been the guru you've been seeking all along.** You just haven't stepped up to claim it.

When you stop seeing yourself as a perpetual student and start seeing yourself as an authority on your own life, you stop living by other people's standards. You begin to define your own path, create your own practices, and set your own rules. **And that's when your journey as a modern guru begins.**

The Key Qualities of a Modern Guru

Now that you're ready to embody the guru mindset, let's break down what that actually looks like in your day-to-day life. I'm talking about the qualities you need to develop and apply to truly step into your own power.

1. **Self-Mastery**

   A true guru doesn't run from their weaknesses. They face them head-on and continuously work to transcend them. You can't teach others if you can't manage your own emotions, your thoughts, and your actions. **Self-mastery** is the foundation. It's the ability to show up with unwavering consistency, regardless of external circumstances.

Here's how to build self-mastery:

- **Practice awareness**: Pay attention to your thoughts and emotions. Become the observer of your own mind.
- **Master your habits**: Create routines that align with your highest values and stick to them.
- **Stay calm under pressure**: Learn how to breathe through stress and respond, not react.

1. **Wisdom**

   A guru doesn't just spout information. They **live their wisdom**. They've learned through experience and self-reflection. They know that wisdom is about seeing the bigger picture and helping others do the same. But it's not enough to learn from books—**you have to learn from life.**

Here's how to cultivate wisdom:

- **Reflect daily**: Spend time each day reflecting on your experiences. What have you learned? How can you apply it to grow?
- **Take ownership of your journey**: Stop blaming circumstances or others for where you are. The guru takes responsibility for their own life.
- **Share your wisdom**: Don't keep it to yourself. Speak, write, or teach in a way that helps others see the truth you've discovered.

1. **Compassion**
   The modern guru leads with compassion. They know that every person is on their own journey, and they don't judge others. **Compassion is the ability to understand and empathize with others' struggles, and to act in a way that uplifts them.**

Here's how to build compassion:

- **Listen deeply**: Be present when people speak. Don't just wait for your turn to talk.
- **Serve selflessly**: Look for opportunities to give without expecting anything in return.
- **Practice forgiveness**: Let go of grudges. Let go of judgments. Compassion means releasing the need to hold on to past hurts.

1. **Presence**
   A guru is present in every moment. They aren't distracted by the noise of the world. They give all of their attention to whoever or whatever is in front of them. **Presence means showing up fully—physically, mentally, and emotionally.**

Here's how to cultivate presence:

- **Be in the moment**: Stop multi-tasking. When you're with someone, be with them completely.

- **Engage your senses**: Use all your senses to connect with the world around you. Feel the air, see the colors, listen to the sounds.
- **Be mindful**: Practice mindfulness every day. Whether you're meditating, walking, or eating—be fully aware of the experience.

1. **Fearlessness**
   A guru doesn't shy away from difficult situations. They face challenges head-on, knowing that they will grow through them. **Fearlessness is not about being without fear; it's about moving forward even when you're scared.**

Here's how to develop fearlessness:

- **Embrace discomfort**: Step out of your comfort zone. The growth you're looking for happens when you're uncomfortable.
- **Take risks**: Take action even if you're uncertain about the outcome. The guru knows that failure is just another lesson.
- **Trust yourself**: Have confidence in your ability to handle whatever comes your way.

Shifting from Follower to Leader

This transition is key: **from follower to leader.** As long as you keep following, you'll never fully step into your power. **Being a leader doesn't mean having a title**; it means living in such a way that others are drawn to you for guidance and inspiration.

The guru doesn't wait for permission to lead. They don't ask, "Do I have the right to lead?" They just lead, because they know that **leadership is not about authority**. It's about showing up consistently with authenticity, wisdom, and a genuine desire to help others.

How do you shift from follower to leader?

- **Own your truth**: Stop looking for external validation. Be true to who you are.

- **Lead by example**: Your actions will speak louder than your words. Be the embodiment of what you believe.
- **Take responsibility**: Leaders take responsibility for their own lives and the impact they have on others. **Own it.**

Becoming the Guru in Your Own Life

To become the guru you seek, you don't have to build an empire or collect followers. You need to live in alignment with your highest self. **You need to show up every day with intention, compassion, wisdom, and authenticity.**

You don't need to make an announcement, you don't need a stage, and you don't need a title. **You need to be you**, fully, unapologetically, and fearlessly. When you embody the guru qualities within yourself, **you inspire others to do the same.**

Start right now. Don't wait for a special moment or a sign. **The time is now.** Every choice you make, every action you take, can be a step toward becoming the guru you are meant to be.

Call to Action

So, what are you waiting for? **You've been training for this your whole life.** Start living as the guru you were always meant to be. Stop following. Start leading. Take ownership of your journey, and create the impact that will echo far beyond your time on this earth.

Your legacy begins now.

Part 4: The Continuous Journey

———

Let's get this straight: **The guru's journey doesn't end.** It doesn't plateau. There's no finish line. If you think for one second that you've "arrived," that you're done growing, then you're missing the whole point. **Mastery is a process, not a destination.** It's about getting better every single day—**not about reaching some magical level of perfection.**

The guru understands this. They know that the path to mastery is constant, ongoing, and never fully complete. And if you want to think like a modern guru, you better get used to the idea that **you are always evolving.** So, stop thinking that once you've learned something, you're set for life. **You're not.** The moment you stop growing is the moment you start decaying.

This is the truth: **Living like a guru isn't a phase you go through.** It's a mindset, a lifestyle, a commitment to continual development. This journey doesn't stop just because you've learned a few tricks or heard some profound insights. You don't just sit back and say, "I've got this." You get up every morning and recommit yourself to being better, doing better, **and serving better.**

The Journey is the Destination

Understand this: The moment you begin thinking like a guru, you've stepped onto a never-ending road. You can't "arrive" at being a guru. **The journey itself is the point. There is no end.** It's not a "one-time achievement" you check off. It's a relentless pursuit of wisdom, self-awareness, and service to others.

Take a step back for a moment. When was the last time you felt like you were truly growing? Like you were challenged to the edge of your limits? That's the kind of growth you need to seek out daily. Every day offers new opportunities to learn, expand, and rise above who you were yesterday.

This journey requires humility. You can't be a guru if you think you've figured it all out. The real guru never stops questioning, never stops seeking, and never stops improving. **You're not here to master everything at once**—you're here to live each moment with purpose, integrity, and deep self-awareness. If you think you've "arrived," you're already slipping.

Self-Awareness is Your Compass

Self-awareness is the most important tool you have on this journey. It's the compass that points you in the right direction. You don't need to seek out some mystical, unattainable wisdom from the outside world. **It's all inside you.** And to access it, you need to build a deep, honest, and continuous awareness of yourself—your thoughts, your reactions, your motives, and your emotions.

The guru lives with an open mind, not closed off by ego or arrogance. Self-awareness means knowing **who you are** and **who you're becoming**. It's about recognizing your strengths and your weaknesses—and having the courage to address them head-on. You're not here to deceive yourself into thinking you're perfect. You're here to expose the truth of who you are so that you can get better.

Actionable Exercise:

- Spend 10 minutes every day in self-reflection. Sit quietly, observe your thoughts, and ask yourself: "What part of myself am I avoiding right now? What do I need to face?" This exercise sharpens your awareness and forces you to confront the areas where you need growth.
- Ask yourself regularly: **"Who am I today?"** Get specific. What are the thoughts, actions, and attitudes you're living by? Are they serving your growth or holding you back?

Purpose, Peace, and Service: The Core Pillars

A modern guru is driven by **purpose**. They don't wander aimlessly through life, hoping for fulfillment. They understand that **purpose is the engine that drives them**—and it should drive you, too. If you don't have a clear sense of purpose, you're not truly living. You're just existing.

Purpose gives you direction, and it keeps you on course when challenges and distractions come your way. It reminds you of why you're doing this work and what it's all for.

At the same time, a guru also cultivates **peace**. **Peace isn't a passive state—it's an active practice.** It's not about waiting for life to give you peace. It's about creating inner peace, no matter what's happening on the outside. You can't teach others if you're constantly in turmoil. Peace is the foundation from which everything else flows.

And the last pillar is **service**. A guru doesn't just work on themselves—they serve others. **Service is the true test of your growth.** If you're only in it for yourself, you'll hit a wall. But if you live with the mindset of serving others, you expand. You become greater than yourself, because you're connected to something bigger.

Actionable Exercise:

- **Define your purpose:** Take some time to write down your purpose in life. Be clear about what you want to create, contribute, or change. Write it down. Make it real. Then check in with that purpose every morning.
- **Create moments of peace:** Practice mindfulness every day. Whether it's through breathing exercises, meditation, or simply being present in the moment, make peace an intentional part of your day.
- **Serve others every day:** Look for ways you can serve. It doesn't have to be grand. It could be offering a kind word, listening to someone who needs to talk, or giving without expectation.

Continuous Growth: The Guru's Mindset

You're not going to master everything all at once. It's not about reaching some point where you can sit back and say, "I've got this." It's about getting better every day. This is the difference between a guru mindset and the average mindset. **The guru knows that growth is a marathon, not a sprint.**

The guru doesn't seek shortcuts. They don't look for a quick fix. They understand that it's the small daily habits that compound over time to create the real change. So stop chasing after miracles. **Focus on the mundane, the ordinary, the consistent actions that bring you closer to mastery every day.**

Here's the bottom line: **You're never "done" with your growth.** The moment you think you've hit the peak is the moment you stop climbing. And if you stop climbing, you start sliding backward.

So what does it look like to keep growing? Here are a few practices to embed into your life:

1. **Stay humble**: Always be willing to learn. The moment you think you know it all, you stop learning.
2. **Embrace failure**: Failure isn't the end. It's a lesson. **You learn more from mistakes than from success.**
3. **Keep a growth mindset**: Focus on development, not perfection. Every day, strive to be a better version of yourself than you were yesterday.
4. **Cultivate gratitude**: A guru is grateful for what they have, even in the toughest moments. Gratitude fuels peace and keeps you grounded in the present.
5. **Teach others**: You learn by teaching. Share your wisdom. Serve others. Teach what you've learned, and you'll deepen your own understanding.

The Final Call: You Are the Guru

You've learned the principles. You've heard the wisdom. Now, it's time to act. **Step into your role as the guru in your own life.** This isn't about grand gestures. It's about living with consistency, purpose, and a relentless commitment to growth.

You are the guru you seek. You've always been.

The question is, will you live that truth every single day? Will you take the journey, commit to the practices, and embrace the endless pursuit of wisdom, service, and self-awareness?

The choice is yours. **The journey continues.** Keep moving forward.

Epilogue: The Journey Never Ends

So, here you are.

You've made it through the pages, absorbed the lessons, and maybe you've even put some of these principles into practice. But I'm going to be straight with you: **this isn't the end.** In fact, it's just the beginning.

You've been given the tools. You've learned the principles. You've got a roadmap to think like a modern guru. But now, it's up to you to walk the path. To **embody** what you've learned. To live it, breathe it, and let it shape every corner of your life.

The truth is, the guru's journey never ends. And neither does yours.

You've tasted the power of self-mastery. You've experienced the fire of resilience. You've glimpsed what it means to live with purpose, to serve with compassion, and to create a legacy that will last long after you're gone. But now it's time to **keep moving**. To keep growing. To keep evolving.

Let me break it down for you: **growth doesn't come from comfort.** It never has, and it never will. If you're comfortable right now, you're likely stuck. You're in a safe space, and that's the opposite of what we're after. **You're here to break through.** To test your limits, to challenge your weaknesses, and to turn every obstacle into an opportunity for growth.

The guru mindset isn't about reaching some final destination, some zen-like state of perfect enlightenment. It's about continually leveling up. Every day is a new chance to step into your power. Every challenge is a new opportunity to refine your character. **Every single moment offers you a choice:** to show up as the best version of yourself, or to stay stuck in old patterns of mediocrity.

If you've read this book and thought to yourself, "I'm going to master my thoughts," "I'm going to live with purpose," or "I'm going to make a real difference in the world," that's great. But here's the kicker: **words are easy. Actions are where the work is.**

It's easy to say you want to be like a guru. It's easy to think, "Yeah, I can do this." But living it—**that's where the rubber meets the road.** It's the small, daily choices that define you. It's how you show up in the face of adversity. It's how you respond when things get hard. How you act when no one is watching. **That's the true measure of a modern guru.**

And here's the reality check: You're not going to get it right every time. You'll slip. You'll fall. You'll have days when you feel like you've taken ten steps backward. But that's the point: **falling is not failing**. It's part of the process. It's part of the refining, the learning, the growing.

Don't expect perfection. Don't expect to reach some static version of yourself that has it all figured out. **Perfection is a myth.** The guru mindset isn't about perfection—it's about progress. It's about waking up every day with the intention to be better than you were yesterday, and doing that day after day, year after year.

Think about it like this: **You are the sculptor, and your life is the marble.** The more you chip away at it, the clearer your true form becomes. The more you shed your old, limiting beliefs, the closer you get to the person you were always meant to be. It's messy. It's uncomfortable. But it's worth it. And each day, that marble gets closer to becoming a masterpiece.

So, what's next for you? What's the next step? How are you going to take what you've learned here and put it into action?

You don't need anyone else to tell you what to do. **You already know.** The wisdom is within you. The strength is within you. The power to create the life you want—it's all within you.

It's time to own it.

It's time to stand in your power.

It's time to show the world what a modern guru looks like in the 21st century.

Be the leader, the warrior, the teacher, and the servant. Be the person who **doesn't wait for things to change**—who changes things. Be the person who shows up with clarity, strength, and purpose. Be the person who stands tall in the face of adversity and keeps going. Be the person who gives without expectation and leads without arrogance.

Because here's the truth: **This is your legacy.**

And it doesn't start in some distant future. It starts **right now**. The choices you make, the actions you take, the mindset you develop—it all creates the life you'll leave behind. **So make it count.**

I'm not here to tell you what to do, but I'll say this: you've got what it takes. You've got the tools. You've got the knowledge. You've got the fire.

So go out there and make it happen. Live like a guru. Think like a guru. Be a guru.

And remember: **The journey never ends.** You've just taken the first step. Keep walking. Keep growing. Keep evolving. The world needs what you have to offer.

Now, get out there and show them.

Appendix 1

Practical Examples and Case Studies: Living the Guru Mindset in the Modern World

The teachings of the modern guru aren't just theoretical. They're practical. They live and breathe in the people around you, in the leaders, the changemakers, and the trailblazers. The principles of spiritual wisdom and self-mastery aren't meant to be confined to temples, ashrams, or retreat centers. They belong in your everyday life: in your office, your relationships, your community, and your most challenging moments.

I could sit here and talk abstractly about what it means to "think like a guru," but I'm not here to feed you concepts. I'm here to show you how this stuff works in the real world. I want to give you examples, stories, and case studies of modern-day gurus—people who live by these principles and demonstrate how they can be embodied in action. These are leaders, activists, entrepreneurs, and spiritual figures whose lives are living proof that the guru mindset is not just something for monks or mystics, but something you can practice, right now, in the hustle of everyday life.

Let's start with a few examples.

1. Elon Musk: Visionary Leadership and the Guru Mindset in Business

Elon Musk might not be the first name that comes to mind when you think of a "spiritual guru," but stick with me. Musk is someone who has reshaped multiple industries. Whether it's space exploration, electric vehicles, or sustainable energy, Musk's work is a perfect example of someone who has radically disrupted norms and approached the world from a place of **visionary leadership** and **self-mastery**.

Musk embodies the guru mindset by focusing on **service to humanity**—his companies are working toward a future of sustainable energy and human survival beyond Earth. But there's another side to Musk that aligns with the guru ethos: his **resilience** in the face of near-total failure. In the early 2000s, his electric car company, Tesla, was on the brink of bankruptcy. Despite that, Musk pushed forward. He invested all his personal money into Tesla and SpaceX, nearly losing everything. He faced criticism, ridicule, and personal challenges.

Here's where the guru mentality really shines. Musk didn't let the failures define him. He didn't hide from adversity—he walked straight into it, with eyes wide open. Like a guru, he was able to detach from the fear of failure and keep his focus on the **long-term mission**. He is living proof that **true mastery is not about avoiding failure but about using failure as a stepping stone** to something greater.

Actionable Insight: Look at Musk's ability to keep pushing forward, even when all odds were stacked against him. Ask yourself: What are the bigger visions or dreams in your life that you've abandoned due to fear of failure or criticism? Write them down. Reconnect with them. You may not be trying to save humanity, but you can still use **resilience** and **purpose-driven action** to power your way through obstacles. Don't let failure stop you—it's just feedback.

2. Brené Brown: Vulnerability and Courage in Leadership

Brené Brown is a research professor and author who has reshaped how we think about leadership, vulnerability, and courage. Her work isn't just academic; it's deeply personal. In her book *Daring Greatly*, Brown explores the idea that the most effective leaders are the ones who embrace vulnerability—who don't hide behind a façade of invulnerability but are willing to show up, **authentically** and **bravely**.

This speaks directly to the guru mindset, especially in leadership. Gurus don't rely on their titles, power, or authority to command respect—they lead by **example**, by showing their **humanity**, and by demonstrating their **willingness to be vulnerable**. The guru doesn't hide from their fears.

Instead, they face them head-on, knowing that vulnerability is a **source of strength**, not weakness.

In her famous TED Talk, Brown recounts a moment when she realized that in order to truly lead, she had to open herself up to discomfort, uncertainty, and vulnerability. She made the conscious choice to take risks and embrace her imperfections—an idea that resonates deeply with the **guru's journey** of **self-acceptance**.

Actionable Insight: Brown's work can inspire you to redefine leadership in your own life. It doesn't matter if you're leading a team at work, a family, or a community project—**vulnerability is a strength**. To embody the guru mindset, try embracing one area of your life where you feel guarded or defensive. Share something personal or uncertain with a trusted colleague, friend, or family member. Let go of the need for perfection and open yourself up. **True leadership** begins when you drop the armor and show your **authentic self.**

3. Malala Yousafzai: Resilience, Compassion, and the Courage to Lead

Malala Yousafzai is the youngest-ever Nobel Prize laureate, an advocate for girls' education, and an activist who has faced more adversity than most people will face in their entire lives. After being shot in the head by the Taliban for her activism, Malala didn't retreat into silence—she emerged as a global force for education, human rights, and empowerment.

What makes Malala's story a modern guru story? It's her ability to blend **compassion**, **courage**, and **service to humanity** into a life of **purpose**. She didn't just survive the violence and trauma—she **transformed** it into a call to action. Her resilience in the face of overwhelming adversity embodies the key qualities of the guru mindset: **a deep sense of mission, an unwavering commitment to justice, and the willingness to make personal sacrifices for the collective good.**

Malala's work and life embody the lesson that **service** isn't just something you do when you're comfortable—it's often something you do **in the face of your own pain** and discomfort. The guru understands that their life is not just about themselves—it's about the service they provide to others, especially those who cannot advocate for themselves.

Actionable Insight: Like Malala, you might find that some of your deepest sources of strength come from your most difficult experiences. Think of a challenge you're currently facing—something that feels almost too big to handle. Now ask yourself: How can you transform this experience into something that serves a greater good? How can you use your **personal challenges** to fuel your **service** to others? Your pain, like Malala's, can become a platform for something much bigger than yourself.

4. Yvon Chouinard: Eco-Conscious Entrepreneurship and the Guru Mindset

Yvon Chouinard is the founder of Patagonia, an outdoor clothing company that has built its brand around environmental sustainability and social responsibility. Chouinard doesn't just sell gear for climbers and adventurers—he's built a **legacy of environmental activism** into the company's DNA. Patagonia is known for its commitment to reducing environmental impact, donating a percentage of profits to environmental causes, and encouraging customers to buy used goods instead of new ones.

Chouinard's approach to business challenges the conventional idea that companies should be solely profit-driven. Like the guru, he operates from a place of deep **integrity**, choosing to prioritize environmental responsibility over short-term financial gain. His actions show that **true success** isn't about maximizing profit at all costs—it's about aligning your work with your **values** and staying true to what's important.

Patagonia has created a **legacy of service** to the planet, and Chouinard's life demonstrates how one can lead in a way that's not just profitable, but also responsible and impactful.

Actionable Insight: Chouinard's example shows that true mastery and leadership are about creating **alignment** between your values and actions. How can you begin to infuse your life and work with more purpose? Identify one area where your actions are currently misaligned with your core values.

Take one step today to bring them back into alignment. Whether it's changing your approach to business, relationships, or daily habits, **integration** of your core values into everything you do is a step toward mastering the guru mindset.

The modern guru mindset is not just about spiritual enlightenment or leadership in a vacuum. It's about **living out your values** in the world—whether you're leading a multi-million-dollar company, fighting for social change, or simply trying to get through your day with integrity. The people I've mentioned here—Musk, Brown, Malala, Chouinard—are all living examples of what happens when you think like a guru and **embrace adversity** with **resilience, service, and compassion.**

The guru mindset isn't an abstract ideal—it's a real-world, down-and-dirty approach to leadership, service, and **purpose-driven action.** You can start practicing it right now, in your life. Find a problem, step into it, and solve it. Build something bigger than yourself. **Start living like the guru you were meant to be.**

Appendix 2

Dealing with Self-Doubt and Inner Criticism: The Guru's Secret Weapon

Let me tell you something straight: **self-doubt is your enemy**. The voice in your head telling you you're not good enough, that you're failing, or that you'll never make it—those voices are nothing more than noise. They are distractions. **They are the lies that keep you small**. The modern guru doesn't listen to that noise. They don't make space for it, because they know that **the only voice that matters is the one that tells them to move forward**—no matter the obstacles.

But here's the problem: that inner critic—the one that undermines you at every turn—is loud. It's persistent. It tells you you're not smart enough, not strong enough, not capable enough to achieve greatness. That voice might even be the loudest voice in your head. It's the same voice that stops you from doing what you know you're capable of. The one that tells you not to speak up, not to take that leap of faith, or not to put your heart on the line. It's easy to get trapped by that voice and believe it's the truth.

But listen up: **it's not the truth.** It's just the old programming talking. It's the fear of failure, the fear of judgment, the fear of the unknown. The more you let that voice control you, the further away you get from your potential. The modern guru knows how to deal with self-doubt. They don't just acknowledge it—they **destroy it.**

The Guru's First Rule: Recognize the Critic for What It Is

You've got to start by understanding this simple truth: **the critic is not you**. It's just a collection of old patterns, beliefs, and fears that you've absorbed from the outside world. It's the voice of the parents who doubted you, the teachers who told you you'd never make it, the colleagues who mocked your ideas, and the countless times you failed and got back up, only to fail again.

That critic is a **story** you've been telling yourself. And right now, you're living out that story. But it's not a reality—it's just a pattern. It's an old, outdated version of yourself trying to keep you safe. And what does **safety** lead to? **Comfort.** And what does comfort lead to? **Stagnation. Mediocrity.**

A guru doesn't buy into the story. A guru doesn't sit back and accept the narrative that says "you're not enough." A guru recognizes the story, names it for what it is, and then **dismisses it**. You must do the same. It's time to stop letting the critic run the show.

Step 1: Self-Compassion – Be Your Own Ally

Self-compassion is your first weapon. Most of us are our harshest critics. If you've ever made a mistake, messed up a project, or experienced failure in some form, how did you treat yourself? Did you beat yourself up? Did you replay the mistake over and over in your head? Did you make it worse by piling on guilt and shame?

If so, stop. Right now. This is a mistake. You are not here to be your own enemy. You're not here to punish yourself for every mistake. You're here to grow. Mistakes are part of the process. You know what they say: **you don't learn to walk by avoiding falling down—you learn to walk by getting up every time you fall.**

Self-compassion means **being kind to yourself** in moments of failure, just like you would be kind to a friend going through a tough time. Instead of beating yourself up for not being perfect, **accept yourself exactly as you are**, flaws and all. The guru does not expect perfection—they expect progress. They don't crush themselves under the weight of self-criticism—they embrace the reality that failure is an integral part of success.

Actionable Exercise: Next time you experience self-doubt, pause for a moment and ask yourself: *If my best friend were here, how would I comfort them right now?* Now, offer that same kindness and compassion to yourself. Write it down. Speak it out loud. Give yourself the permission to be human.

Step 2: Reframe Your Thoughts – Turn the Critic's Lies Into Fuel

Your inner critic isn't a wall—it's a door. It's trying to teach you something, even though it's often wrong in how it presents itself. When you feel the sharp sting of self-doubt, instead of letting it paralyze you, **reframe it**. That's the key to defeating the critic. Take that negative thought—"I'm not good enough," for example—and flip it on its head.

Reframe: "I may not have the answers right now, but I'm fully capable of figuring this out. I've done it before, and I'll do it again."

The critic tells you you're not capable, and the guru responds by saying, "That's an old story. Let me show you what I can really do." When the critic tells you that you'll fail, the guru says, "Failure isn't the end—it's feedback. It's data. And I can use it to improve."

It's a **shift in mindset** from one of **limitation** to one of **empowerment**. The guru doesn't see challenges as insurmountable obstacles—they see them as opportunities for growth. They see obstacles as chances to step up and show what they're made of.

Actionable Exercise: Next time you hear the voice of self-doubt telling you that you can't do something, immediately challenge it. Write down the negative thought and then **counter it** with a reframe that empowers you. Ask yourself: *What's the evidence that I can succeed? What's the next small step I can take?*

Step 3: Affirmations and Mindfulness – Rewire Your Brain

If you want to defeat self-doubt, you've got to rewire your brain. The neural pathways that reinforce negativity can be **reprogrammed** with consistent, conscious practice. **Affirmations** are one of the most powerful tools for this. They work because they retrain your mind to focus on what is true about you, rather than what you fear.

A guru doesn't stand around waiting for others to tell them they're enough. A guru **tells themselves every day** that they are enough, that they are capable, that they are worthy of success. The guru **reaffirms** their mission, their worth, and their power, each and every day.

But words alone aren't enough. You need to **feel the words**. This is where **mindfulness** comes in. Mindfulness teaches you to observe your thoughts without getting caught up in them. It helps you recognize when your inner critic is running the show so you can step back, breathe, and **choose your response**.

Actionable Exercise: Start your day with a series of affirmations that counter the self-doubt. Look in the mirror and repeat these affirmations with conviction:

- "I am capable of overcoming any challenge."
- "I am worthy of success and happiness."
- "I trust in my ability to figure things out." As you say these words, close your eyes for a moment and **feel** them. Let them sink in. Take a few deep breaths, and **visualize yourself living these affirmations**. See yourself acting with confidence and self-assurance.

Step 4: Mindfulness-Based Cognitive Behavioral Techniques (CBT) – Take Control of Your Thoughts

Mindfulness and cognitive behavioral therapy (CBT) techniques work together to help you **identify** and **disrupt** negative thought patterns. CBT teaches you to recognize when your mind is spiraling into self-doubt and to **interrupt** that spiral with more constructive, reality-based thinking.

A guru knows that **their thoughts are not facts**. When a thought pops into your head like, "I'm not good enough," don't just accept it as truth. Instead, **question it**. Is this thought grounded in reality? What evidence do I have that this is true? More often than not, you'll find that your inner critic is based on **assumptions**, **fears**, or **past experiences**—not on facts.

Actionable Exercise: Use CBT techniques to challenge negative thoughts. When you notice self-doubt creeping in, ask yourself:

- What is the evidence for this thought?
- What's the worst-case scenario, and how would I handle it?
- What's the best-case scenario, and what's the most likely outcome?

By repeatedly challenging negative thoughts, you start to **retrain your mind** to focus on what's real, not on what your inner critic is telling you.

Mastering the Inner Critic

You've got the tools now. **Self-compassion** to soften the harsh voice of the critic. **Reframing** to turn doubts into fuel. **Affirmations and mindfulness** to rewire your brain for success. And **CBT techniques** to disrupt the negative thought patterns that try to drag you down.

The guru mindset isn't about never feeling doubt—it's about **handling it like a pro**. It's about **knowing that doubt is just a part of the process**, not the end of the road. The modern guru **moves through self-doubt**, they don't let it paralyze them. They **act anyway**.

Now it's your turn. When that inner critic shows up—and it will—don't listen to it. **Shut it down.**

Appendix 3

The Importance of Self-Care and Balance – The Guru's Secret Weapon

Listen up, because I'm going to tell you something critical—**you cannot pour from an empty cup.** You can't give what you don't have. And if you're running on fumes, burnt out, and overwhelmed, don't even think about leading, teaching, or showing up with the wisdom you claim to have. A real modern guru knows this. **They know that balance isn't a luxury—it's a necessity.** They understand that to serve others, they first must take care of themselves.

It's easy to fall into the trap of thinking that the path of a guru is all about being selfless, always giving, always serving. You might think, "If I'm not working nonstop, I'm being lazy," or "If I'm not helping everyone, I'm failing." That's the trap. And it will lead to **burnout, exhaustion,** and **resentment**—none of which have any place in a guru's life.

So here's the cold hard truth: **The guru who doesn't practice self-care is no guru at all.**

You're here to make an impact, to leave a legacy, to become the person others can turn to when they need wisdom and guidance. But how are you supposed to do that if you're drained, depleted, and drowning in stress? The energy you give others must come from an abundant, well-maintained reservoir inside you. If you're running on empty, everything you give will be shallow, strained, and half-hearted.

Self-Care Is Not a Luxury—It's a Requirement

If you think that self-care is selfish, you're dead wrong. Self-care isn't about being indulgent. It's not about taking bubble baths all day or going on spa retreats (although those can be nice). It's about making sure that your **mind,**

body, and soul are operating at full capacity. It's about **setting boundaries**, protecting your time, and ensuring that your inner resources are replenished, so you can show up for others in a meaningful way.

Gurus are not just passive fountains of wisdom. They are human beings who know the importance of **nourishing their mental health, prioritizing their emotional well-being,** and **giving their bodies the care and rest they need to function**. Without this, they become ineffective, irrelevant, and unproductive. A modern guru **knows** that if they don't take care of themselves first, they'll have nothing left to give.

If you're thinking, "I don't have time for that" or "That's not practical," it's time to take a step back and re-evaluate. **Your well-being is the foundation for everything else in your life.** Without it, you'll burn out, crash, and become a shadow of the person you know you could be. **Take care of yourself, or nothing else matters.**

Mental Wellness: The Guru's Mindset

Let's talk about mental health for a minute. You can't talk about being a modern guru without addressing your mental state. This is where **mindfulness, meditation,** and **emotional regulation** come in. Mental clarity is a huge part of the guru mindset. The ability to stay calm in chaos, to think clearly under pressure, and to maintain emotional stability is what separates the amateurs from the pros. **Mental wellness is a non-negotiable.**

A modern guru isn't swayed by every external circumstance. They don't get dragged into emotional rollercoasters. They **hold their center**—not because they're perfect, but because they've practiced doing so. They've cultivated an inner peace and resilience that's impenetrable by outside noise. When you're mentally well, you can handle the stress of life without it unraveling you. You can **make decisions from a place of calm** rather than reactive panic.

Actionable Tip: If you want to embody this kind of mental toughness, start with meditation. Even 10 minutes a day can make a massive difference in your ability to stay centered and present. Focus on your breath. Notice the thoughts that come up, but don't engage with them. Let them pass. Over time, this practice will help you detach from the noise of your mind and develop the mental clarity that the guru embodies.

Emotional Regulation: Mastering Your Inner State

You cannot be a modern guru without learning how to regulate your emotions. Here's the thing: **emotions are not facts**. They're responses. They're signals. But they don't have to dictate your actions or cloud your judgment. Emotional regulation is the art of observing your emotions without getting swept away by them.

A guru doesn't lose control when things don't go as planned. They don't react impulsively. Instead, they **pause**, they **reflect**, and they **respond** with intention. Their emotions are under control, not the other way around.

Practical Exercise: The next time you feel anger, frustration, or anxiety building up inside you, stop. Close your eyes for a moment, take a deep breath, and ask yourself: *What am I really feeling? What's underneath this emotion?* Often, the emotion is a surface reaction, and when you dig deeper, you'll uncover the root cause—whether it's fear, insecurity, or something else. When you identify the root, you can address it, rather than letting it control you.

Don't let your emotions drive the bus. The guru knows that while emotions are inevitable, **reaction is a choice**.

Physical Wellness: The Body Is the Temple

Let's not sugarcoat this—your body is your **vehicle** for everything in life. If your body is run down, sick, or broken, it's going to be pretty damn hard to serve others. **Your physical health is directly tied to your ability to perform in every area of your life.** You can't talk about wisdom, leadership, or spiritual insight when you can barely keep your eyes open or your back isn't functioning properly.

The modern guru treats their body as sacred. They feed it well, exercise it regularly, and make sure it gets the rest it needs. Without this foundation of physical health, everything else will fall apart. **Your energy is limited**, and you need to be mindful of how you're using it.

If you want to serve others at your highest level, **you need to treat your body with respect**. That means taking care of it. Eating nutritious food, exercising regularly, and getting enough rest. It's not about looking a certain way or achieving some physical ideal—it's about making sure you can function at your best, for yourself and for others.

Sleep: The Ultimate Recharge

I'm going to say this again, because it's critical: **Sleep is non-negotiable**. You want to talk about peak performance? You want to be a modern guru? You need to **get quality sleep**. Without it, you're not functioning at full capacity. Your brain won't be sharp, your emotions will be on a rollercoaster, and your body will start to break down.

The modern guru knows that sleep is **essential** to mental and physical health. You can't just push through exhaustion and expect to be a rockstar. You need **rest**. And not just any rest—good, restorative sleep. Sleep is when your body repairs itself, your brain consolidates memories, and your energy reserves are replenished.

Sleep hygiene is a real thing. Don't play with it. Prioritize sleep like it's your most important mission. Set a sleep schedule. Avoid screens before bed. Create a calming pre-sleep routine. These are simple practices that can drastically improve your life.

Setting Boundaries: Protect Your Energy

Listen closely: **If you don't set boundaries, you'll burn out**. If you let people take advantage of your time, your energy, and your resources without saying "no," you're setting yourself up for failure. Boundaries are not about being rude or selfish—they're about protecting your energy so that you can give **more effectively**.

The guru sets firm boundaries. They **protect their time** like a fortress. They know that if they say yes to everything, they'll be spreading themselves too thin, and eventually, they won't be able to show up fully for anything.

Actionable Exercise: Start practicing saying "no." It doesn't have to be aggressive or defensive. It can be as simple as saying, "I'm unable to take that on right now." Protect your time. Protect your energy. That's how you stay in the game long term.

Conclusion: Recharge to Serve

In a world that's constantly demanding more, the modern guru knows that their power lies in their ability to **balance their own needs with their desire to serve**. They are the embodiment of self-care, maintaining physical, mental, and emotional health so that they can show up with wisdom, energy, and presence. They take care of themselves because they know that **only from a place of fullness can they truly serve others**.

Now get to work. Protect your energy. Practice self-care. Prioritize balance. Because the world needs you at your best—and that starts with you taking care of yourself first. Don't wait until you're running on empty. Start today.

Appendix 4

The Role of Relationships in the Guru's Journey

Listen up, because this is important. You want to be a modern guru? You think it's all about having profound insights, delivering powerful teachings, and leading others to greatness? Think again. **It's about relationships.**

That's right—if you want to be a real guru, you need to master not just yourself, but your interactions with others. Because no matter how wise or skilled you are, **without healthy, meaningful relationships**, your influence will be limited. If you want to create a legacy that lasts, your relationships are the soil that will grow the seeds of your impact.

Being a guru isn't about sitting in a cave, disconnected from the world. No, it's about **being deeply connected** to the people around you. It's about understanding how to communicate, how to serve, how to lead by example, and—most importantly—how to navigate the complex, sometimes toxic, dynamics that exist between people.

You think relationships are just a nice-to-have in this journey of self-mastery? **Wrong.** They're **core** to the process. So buckle up, because we're about to dive deep into how the guru mindset transforms your ability to deal with everyone around you, whether they're family, friends, colleagues, or even strangers.

The Guru and Healthy Relationships

The modern guru understands that their journey of self-mastery cannot be isolated from the relationships they cultivate. The path to wisdom, mastery, and peace is not only an individual pursuit. It's a **collective** effort. Whether it's mentoring someone, collaborating with others, or dealing with friends and family, every interaction shapes who you are. **And that's the point.**

Let's start with the basics. **Healthy relationships require trust, respect, and clear communication.** You want to be a guru? You need to embody these principles in your everyday life. Trust isn't something you just *hope* to develop over time—it's something you build through your actions. Respect isn't a given; you have to demonstrate it. And communication? **If you can't communicate with clarity, compassion, and precision, you're not leading anyone.**

Here's the kicker: the modern guru doesn't sit on a pedestal. They're **in the trenches**. They're engaged. They're human. They face the same relationship challenges as anyone else—**but** they know how to navigate them in ways that promote growth and mutual respect.

Leading by Example

If you want to lead, you need to **set the standard**. You can't expect others to behave in ways you aren't willing to model yourself. The guru is a living example of the values they teach. If you talk about compassion, then show it. If you talk about integrity, then live it. If you preach communication, then practice it.

You think you can lead by telling people what to do while doing something entirely different yourself? **Forget it.** If you want to lead in the guru's way, your life needs to be a walking, talking example of the principles you preach. **This means no double standards.** If you expect your team to be punctual, you better be the first one in the room. If you want respect, you better give it first.

And you can't expect people to follow your lead if you're not showing up with **emotional intelligence**. A guru knows when to push, when to pull back, and when to listen. Emotional intelligence isn't about being nice all the time—it's about **being aware** of how others are feeling and adjusting your approach to meet them where they are. If you're a guru, your ability to read the room and adapt your message accordingly is your **superpower**.

Navigating Toxic Relationships

Not every relationship is going to be smooth sailing. The real world is full of toxic people, negative energy, and difficult dynamics. **So what?** That's part of the deal. If you want to be a guru, you need to know how to deal with toxic people without losing your center or compromising your integrity.

A guru doesn't let toxic energy drag them down. They don't get involved in petty arguments or engage in drama. Instead, they **set boundaries**. They know when to walk away and when to stand their ground. **They protect their peace**, and they're unshakable in that commitment.

Toxic relationships can be draining, but here's the thing: **they're a lesson.** They show you what to avoid, what not to tolerate, and they teach you how to assert yourself. But, and this is key—**don't stay stuck in these relationships**. If someone is actively toxic, you have a duty to protect your energy by either confronting the issue or cutting ties.

A modern guru knows how to **manage** these relationships without getting sucked into them. It's about **detachment**, not disengagement. You don't need to be involved in someone's mess, but you can still offer clarity, empathy, and guidance from a distance.

The Power of Collaboration

You're not in this alone. If you want to be a modern guru, you need to **collaborate**. This isn't a solo mission. Gurus build teams. They bring together people with complementary skills and strengths to create something greater than what they could do on their own.

A guru leads a tribe, not a solo venture. They understand that collaboration is about **leveraging the strengths of others** to amplify the mission. You can't do everything yourself, and you shouldn't try. The power of teamwork is that **together, you can go further**. This is why the guru mindset thrives in collaborative environments—it recognizes that the best results come from **collective effort**.

If you're working with others, you need to **let go of control**. You've got to be willing to listen, be flexible, and give others the freedom to contribute their ideas. The guru knows when to step back and let others take the lead. When you empower others, you build their confidence, and you build a stronger team.

Compassionate Communication

You want to be a modern guru? **Learn how to communicate like one.** Most people suck at communication. They're passive-aggressive. They don't say what they mean, and they don't listen fully. They jump to conclusions, assume things, and let emotions drive their words. **Stop it.**

The guru's communication is clear, direct, and compassionate. When they speak, they do so with the intention of creating understanding, not creating conflict. They ask questions to understand, and they listen to respond, not just to reply. Compassionate communication is about acknowledging the humanity of the other person. Even when you disagree, you communicate with respect and a willingness to understand.

Here's the test: The next time you have a tough conversation, make it your goal to **listen more than you speak**. Try to truly understand the other person's point of view, even if you don't agree. When you speak, do so with compassion and respect. Practice this, and you'll notice how much smoother your relationships become.

Practical Exercises for Improving Communication and Emotional Intelligence

1. Active Listening: Next time you're in a conversation, focus entirely on what the other person is saying—without planning your response while they're speaking. Pause. Reflect. Repeat back what they said in your own words to make sure you understood it correctly.

2. Emotional Check-In: Before responding in any emotionally charged situation, check in with yourself. Ask: *How am I feeling right now? What am I really reacting to?* Taking a moment to understand your own emotions before responding will give you the space to communicate more effectively.

3. Set Boundaries with Compassion: Practice saying "no" with kindness. If someone is asking too much of you or violating your boundaries, learn to assert yourself without aggression or guilt. "I'm not able to take that on right now, but I appreciate you asking."

4. Reflective Journaling: At the end of each day, write down your interactions with others. Did you communicate effectively? Did you lead by example? Did you set healthy boundaries? Reflecting on your communication will help you refine your approach.

Conclusion: Relationships Are Your Greatest Opportunity for Growth

Listen carefully: **Relationships are not a distraction from your guru journey; they are the journey**. If you want to be a modern guru, you have to understand that your growth is intertwined with your interactions with others. You can't master yourself in a vacuum. Relationships challenge you, teach you, and **hold up a mirror** to the areas of yourself that need work.

So, don't avoid the tough conversations. Don't shy away from people who challenge you. And, most importantly, don't try to go it alone. Build your tribe, communicate with clarity and compassion, and lead by example. **That's how you'll make a real impact in the world.**

Get out there. Start improving your relationships. Your mission depends on it.

Appendix 5

Spirituality vs. Practical Action – Bridging the Gap

You want to be a modern guru? Fine. But here's the cold, hard truth: **spirituality alone is worthless if it doesn't get you off your ass and into action**. You can meditate for hours, read all the books, and chant every mantra in the world, but if it doesn't translate into what you're doing every damn day, it's nothing but fluffy nonsense. You can sit on the mountain, or you can make a real impact. But don't fool yourself into thinking that *thinking* like a guru is enough. **You need to act like one.**

I get it. You're looking for a shortcut to wisdom, something you can apply right away. You want to know how to take these deep, spiritual truths and put them to work in your life. I hear you. This is the disconnect that trips people up, every single time. The gap between the lofty ideals of spirituality and the gritty, messy world of practical action is where most people get stuck. And most of them stay stuck. They think the two can't coexist. They think spirituality means being passive, contemplative, or "non-doing." **Wrong.**

Here's the deal: the real power of spirituality is in how you live it. **Every single moment of your life can be a reflection of the spiritual wisdom you claim to follow.** That means no more separating the "spiritual" part of you from the "practical" part of you. You need to fuse them, seamlessly, so that what you do in the world is an expression of your deepest beliefs. **This isn't about balance, it's about integration.** Spiritual wisdom without real-world application is just a hobby. The modern guru doesn't just *talk* spirituality, they live it. They *embody* it.

So, let's cut the crap. You're going to have to get your hands dirty. You're going to have to take what you've learned and use it in the world. This isn't about making your life easier or more comfortable—it's about using spiritual principles as a foundation for how you navigate life's challenges. Are you ready? Because this is how you **bridge the gap** between spirituality and practical action.

Step 1: Set Clear Intentions

Listen to me: You want to take control of your life? **Set intentions**. It's not enough to wake up and hope things work out. The modern guru knows exactly what they're working toward. They don't just wish for success, they **intend** it.

This isn't some fluffy, feel-good "manifestation" nonsense. Setting clear intentions is about getting crystal clear on what you want and then aligning everything you do to get there. It's about creating a mental blueprint for your life, and then executing on it every day. If you're serious about integrating spirituality and action, you need to start each day by defining what you stand for and what you're working to achieve. **No vagueness.**

When you set intentions, you're putting the spiritual principle of **purpose** into action. If your goal is to serve others, to live with integrity, to be present, or to manifest abundance, your intentions need to reflect that. Each day should begin with a purpose that guides everything you do. This is the foundation of *practical* spirituality.

Here's how to do it:

- **Write down your intention for the day**: What is the one thing you want to accomplish today that aligns with your higher purpose? It could be something small—like bringing mindfulness into every conversation—or something bigger, like taking a tangible step toward a personal goal.
- **Be specific**: Don't just say, "I want to be more mindful today." Say, "I will actively practice listening to others without interrupting, and bring my full presence to every conversation."
- **Connect it to a bigger vision**: Your intention isn't just about today. It's about where you're headed. Align your actions with the bigger mission you've set for your life.

Step 2: Use Rituals to Guide Your Day

You're not going to just wake up and *poof*—become a guru. You need routines. You need rituals. You need something that anchors you to your spiritual path every single day. The modern guru **ritualizes their life**. From how they wake up to how they end their day, everything is deliberate.

A ritual is not just some "spiritual fluff." It's a physical action that reminds you of your purpose. It brings focus. It brings clarity. It aligns your mind with your body. You need to treat the most important parts of your day—the way you wake up, the way you eat, the way you rest—like sacred moments that set the tone for everything else.

Here's how to get started:

- **Morning ritual**: Start your day with intention. You're not checking emails or scrolling social media. You're not letting the chaos of the world dictate your energy. Instead, you're getting grounded. You might meditate for 5 minutes, do some deep breathing, or journal about what's important to you today. Whatever it is, you're making sure that **your energy is aligned** with your spiritual purpose before you dive into the world.
- **Meal rituals**: Don't just shove food into your face while you work or watch TV. **Eat mindfully.** Make your meals a reflection of self-care and gratitude. This isn't just about nourishment; it's about honoring your body as the temple it is.
- **Evening ritual**: At the end of the day, take time to reflect. How did you align with your intentions? Did you fall short? What could you do differently tomorrow? Use this time to check in with yourself and **reset** for the next day. You don't leave your spirituality at the door when the day is over. You reinforce it.

Step 3: Align Actions with Principles

Spirituality isn't about feeling good all the time. **It's about acting from your highest self.** You can't say you believe in integrity and then cut corners in business. You can't say you believe in service and then avoid helping someone in need. The modern guru's actions **always** reflect their values.

This is the ultimate test. Every decision you make throughout the day is an opportunity to either **align** with your spiritual principles or go against them. Every conversation, every business decision, every choice you make about how to treat people—**it all comes down to action**. Are your actions aligned with your deepest spiritual truths, or are they just what's easy or convenient?

Here's what to do:

- **Live by your principles**: Identify the core values that define you as a modern guru. Integrity. Service. Compassion. Humility. Whatever it is, **live those values** in every action you take. Don't just talk about them—be them. Let your actions speak louder than your words.
- **Use small daily actions to reinforce your mission**: When faced with a choice, pause and ask yourself, "Is this aligned with my higher purpose?" Whether it's responding to an email, dealing with a tough situation at work, or interacting with a stranger, **make sure your actions match your spiritual commitments**.
- **Take responsibility**: If something goes wrong, don't blame others. Own it. You're the one responsible for your actions, your life, and your mission. A guru doesn't point fingers; they take full responsibility.

Step 4: Stay Grounded in Challenges

Here's the reality: the world is a mess. People are chaotic. Situations are tough. **The path of the modern guru is not an easy one.** So, how do you stay grounded when things fall apart, when people push your buttons, when everything feels like a storm?

You remember your purpose. You don't lose yourself in the chaos. You don't get swept up by negativity. Instead, you stay centered. **Your spiritual practices are what keep you grounded** when life gets hard. Meditation, mindfulness, and reflective practices are not just for calm days—they're your survival kit for when everything is falling apart.

In moments of stress or frustration, stop. Breathe. Center yourself. You are not at the mercy of the world's chaos. You control how you respond.

Conclusion: The Integration of Spirituality and Action

You want to be a guru? Great. But you need to understand this: spirituality isn't a passive state. It's an **active, living** part of who you are. Spirituality without action is like a car without wheels—it doesn't go anywhere. So, take your wisdom and get into motion. Set your intentions, use rituals, align your actions with your values, and stay grounded when challenges arise. This is how you live your life as a modern guru.

Stop waiting for the perfect moment. Start now. Your life is already your spiritual practice. Make it count.

Appendix 6

Addressing Modern Challenges – Keeping the Guru Mindset in a World of Distractions

Alright, listen up. You're living in a world that's constantly demanding your attention. You're bombarded with information, opinions, and notifications at all hours. Everyone's got something to say. Everyone wants a piece of you. Your phone is buzzing, your inbox is overflowing, and the pressure to keep up is relentless. Social media feeds you the illusion of progress, while simultaneously draining you of your energy. **The modern world is a battlefield, and if you're not careful, it'll chew you up and spit you out.**

So, what does the modern guru do? How do you navigate this chaos without losing yourself? **How do you stay grounded, stay true to your values, and keep your energy in check, even when the whole world is pulling you in different directions?**

Here's the deal: **The modern guru knows that distractions are the enemy.** You can't afford to let the noise of the world drown out your purpose. If you want to live a life of clarity, focus, and impact, you need to learn how to **protect your energy** and keep your mind sharp. And that's exactly what we're going to tackle here—how to stay true to your guru mindset amidst all the noise, and how to cut through the distractions that are only serving to derail your mission.

1. The Problem: The Age of Distraction

Social media. Notifications. Instant gratification. The sheer volume of information coming at us every minute of every day is unprecedented. Your attention is being sold to the highest bidder, and if you're not careful, it will get hijacked before you even realize it.

I want you to look at your life right now. **How much of your day is spent reacting to things outside of you?** Responding to emails, scrolling through your feeds, jumping from one task to the next, chasing dopamine hits with every like, retweet, or notification? If you're honest with yourself, it's probably way more than you'd like to admit.

This is not just a productivity issue; it's a **spiritual issue**. Every time you let your attention wander to the next thing, the next shiny object, or the next external validation, you're abandoning your center. You're letting external forces dictate how you feel, what you think, and what you do. The guru doesn't live like this. **The guru takes control of their attention**. They know that where their focus goes, their energy flows.

The world doesn't care about your peace. Social media doesn't care about your mission. If you don't set boundaries and take charge of your attention, you'll be a puppet to the modern world.

2. The Guru Mindset: Focus, Boundaries, and Self-Control

The modern guru is laser-focused. Their attention is their most valuable resource. They don't get pulled in every direction. They don't mindlessly scroll through their feed, comparing their life to others. They don't waste hours jumping between a hundred different tabs, trying to stay on top of the latest news. The guru knows that attention is **intention**.

If you're serious about adopting a guru mindset, it starts with this: **You must control your attention.** This is non-negotiable. Here's how you do it:

A. Set Boundaries

I know, it sounds simple. But it's one of the most powerful things you can do to reclaim your energy. **Set clear boundaries** for how you interact with technology, social media, and other people. You can't afford to be on call 24/ 7. Your mind is not a free-for-all.

- **Phone boundaries**: If you're checking your phone every five minutes, stop. Set time blocks. Decide when you will check your email, your texts, or your social media, and stick to it. **This is critical for keeping your energy high** and your mind clear. You don't need to react to every ping and buzz that comes your way.

- **Social media boundaries**: Social media is a beast. It's engineered to keep you hooked, to make you feel inadequate, to feed your FOMO (Fear of Missing Out). **Do a digital detox.** Start by unfollowing accounts that don't align with your values or that don't inspire you. You don't need to follow everyone. You don't need to consume every post. You need to create space for the things that matter, and that doesn't mean mindlessly scrolling through other people's lives. **This is your life.** Be deliberate about what you consume.

- **Work-life boundaries**: It's not just about cutting out distractions from social media or your phone. You need boundaries in your work life too. If you're a workaholic, if you're constantly "on" and never unplugging, that's a recipe for burnout. **A guru knows when to step away** from their work. They know when to recharge, when to rest, and when to focus on something else. Respect your need for space.

B. Master Your Attention

If you're constantly distracted, it's hard to hear your inner voice. It's hard to get clarity. **You need to train your attention** like a muscle. Meditation is one of the best ways to do this. But beyond meditation, it's about how you move through your day. How present are you? How often do you find yourself mentally checked out while you're doing something?

Start by **practicing mindfulness**. Stay present with whatever you're doing. Whether you're writing an email, having a conversation, or taking a walk—be all in. This is how you bring your spiritual practice into the real world. The guru knows that life is happening right now, not in the past, not in the future. Stay engaged with **the present moment.**

C. Reclaim Your Energy

Social media, news, and constant notifications are energy drains. They feed you an endless stream of external noise, and you're not even aware of how much they're pulling from you. If you're serious about becoming a modern guru, **you must protect your energy**. Here's how:

- **Digital detox**: Schedule time each day to disconnect completely. Turn off your phone. Log out of your email. Don't check social media. Use that time to focus on yourself. Read a book. Meditate. Go for a walk. Spend time with loved ones. The more you unplug, the more you recharge.

- **Energy audits**: Look at the people, situations, and media you interact with daily. Are they feeding you positive energy or draining it? Are you spending time with people who elevate you, or people who leave you feeling exhausted? **Cut out the energy vampires**. Protect your emotional and mental resources like the treasure they are.

- **Rest and recovery**: Don't treat sleep or rest as optional. **You can't perform at your best if you're burnt out.** Rest is an act of self-respect. Make sure you're getting enough sleep, taking breaks during the day, and giving your body the nourishment it needs.

3. How to Apply the Guru Mindset to Modern Challenges

Now, let's get practical. The world is loud. The demands are high. The pressure is constant. But here's how the modern guru faces all of this:

A. Make Time for Quiet

Every guru, whether ancient or modern, has had one thing in common: **They spent time in silence.** In today's world, silence feels like a luxury. But you need it. You need that quiet time to reconnect with your inner self and to reflect on your purpose. Find ways to create moments of silence in your day. Even if it's just 10 minutes in the morning before the world wakes up, use it to center yourself.

B. Focus on Service, Not Comparison

Social media thrives on comparison. People flaunt their "perfect" lives, their vacations, their accomplishments. Don't fall for the trap. The guru is focused on **service, not self-promotion**. If you're in this to make a difference, don't waste your time comparing your journey to someone else's highlight reel. **Your journey is unique.** Focus on what you can give, not what you can get. That's how you remain grounded in your values.

C. Simplify Your Life

The modern world is cluttered. Mentally, physically, and emotionally. **The guru keeps things simple.** Eliminate the unnecessary distractions. Declutter your space, your schedule, your mind. The simpler your life, the more room you have for clarity, focus, and action.

4. Practical Takeaways

- **Set clear boundaries** with technology, social media, and work.
- **Practice mindfulness** and keep your attention on the present moment.
- **Reclaim your energy** with daily digital detoxes and by protecting your mental and emotional resources.
- **Create time for silence** to reconnect with your inner self.
- **Focus on service** instead of comparison.
- **Simplify your life** by eliminating unnecessary distractions.

Conclusion: Mastering the Modern World

The modern world will never stop throwing distractions at you. But the modern guru doesn't let that control them. **You decide what to focus on. You decide what to allow into your life.** Don't be a slave to the noise. Take control. The more you protect your attention, the more you'll be able to channel your energy into what truly matters—your mission, your purpose, and the people you serve.

The world is chaotic, but **you don't have to be**. Stay grounded. Stay focused. And remember: **The guru's power comes from within.**

Appendix 7

Building a Personal Practice and Rituals – The Key to Sustaining the Guru Mindset

Alright, pay attention, because if you think you can just flip a switch and *bam*, you're a guru, you're wrong. **Being a guru is not a one-time decision.** It's a daily commitment. Every day, you must show up for yourself. No one's going to do it for you. You don't just think like a guru, **you live like one.** You embody the mindset, the discipline, and the spirit. You **create a daily practice** that not only keeps you grounded but also propels you forward.

Let me put it bluntly: **Without a personal practice, you'll fall off track.** If you're trying to stay focused, stay aligned, and stay true to your mission, you need a routine. This isn't just about checking off boxes or following a series of steps. **It's about creating a structure that reinforces who you are and what you're becoming.**

Now, let me show you how to build that practice, because without it, you're just going through the motions. The guru knows that consistency is the foundation of everything. Rituals—*personal rituals*—are non-negotiable if you want to stay in the game long-term.

1. The Power of Rituals

Let's start with this: **rituals are the backbone of mastery.** They are what keep you consistent, what give you purpose, and what keep you grounded in your values. The moment you wake up, the moment you go to bed, and every single moment in between—**your rituals will define you.** The guru mindset isn't something you flip on and off like a light switch. It's a lifestyle, a constant evolution.

Do you have a morning ritual? An evening ritual? Do you have time carved out for reflection, for growth, for setting your intentions? Or do you simply react to whatever comes your way?

A guru's rituals serve as reminders—**reminders of their purpose, their mission, and their spiritual commitment**. They anchor the mind in the present moment and align actions with intention. Without them, you're just reacting to the world around you instead of **leading** it.

2. Crafting Your Morning Ritual – Setting the Tone for the Day

How you start your day matters. **The first hour of your day sets the tone for everything that follows.** If you wake up and dive straight into emails, social media, or your to-do list, you're already letting the world dictate your priorities. You're starting the day as a reactor, not a creator. You're starting from a place of distraction.

Let's fix that.

Step 1: Wake Up Early

No, you're not waking up at 4:30 AM to become a motivational quote. But you do need to wake up early enough that you're not rushed. That you can take your time. **A guru doesn't hit snooze and roll out of bed in a panic.** They wake up early enough to take control of the day.

Step 2: Hydrate and Move

Drink a glass of water. Your body needs hydration to function at its peak. After that, **move**. It doesn't matter whether you do yoga, a few stretches, a short walk, or even a short burst of high-intensity exercise—get your blood flowing. Physical movement wakes up the body, clears the mind, and gets you ready to face the day.

Step 3: Meditation or Mindfulness Practice

Now that your body is awake, it's time for your mind. **Meditation is the anchor for your day.** You don't need to sit in silence for an hour, but even 10-15 minutes of mindfulness or meditation will reset your focus and set you on the path of calm. Focus on your breath, on gratitude, or on an intention for the day.

If you're struggling to quiet your mind, **focus on your breath.** Just inhale deeply for a count of four, hold for four, and exhale for four. Keep repeating this, and your mind will start to settle.

Step 4: Set Your Intention for the Day

What's your goal for today? What do you want to accomplish? What do you need to remind yourself of? **Write it down.** No, really. Write it down. Even a single sentence can change the trajectory of your day. It could be something simple like, "Today I will stay focused on my mission," or "I will lead with compassion and strength." You need to create that mental anchor.

Step 5: Ritualize a Morning Practice

You need something consistent. **A morning ritual needs repetition.** It needs to become a habit. For some, it could be as simple as reading a passage from a book that inspires you, doing a short breathing practice, or setting your daily goals. You must create something you can lean on.

Actionable Exercise for Your Morning Ritual:

1. Wake up 15-30 minutes earlier.
2. Drink a glass of water.
3. Spend 10-15 minutes in meditation or mindfulness.
4. Write down your intention for the day.
5. Move your body (stretch, walk, or exercise).

3. Crafting Your Evening Ritual – Closing the Loop on Your Day

You think your day ends when you put your head on the pillow. **Wrong.** The way you end your day affects the quality of your sleep and the mindset you wake up with. The evening ritual should be just as intentional as your morning routine.

Step 1: Review Your Day

Take 5-10 minutes to reflect on what you did. **What went well?** What didn't? This isn't about beating yourself up; it's about learning and growing. Acknowledge your wins. If you missed the mark, be honest with yourself. This is where you can identify growth opportunities.

Step 2: Journal for Insight

Journaling is a guru's secret weapon. It's your opportunity to reflect, to record what you've learned, and to **get the clutter out of your mind**. Whether you write about your thoughts, your challenges, or insights you gained throughout the day, journaling is your mental decluttering session. **Get the crap out of your head so you can sleep peacefully**.

Here's a simple journaling exercise: **Write down three things you're grateful for**. It might sound cliché, but gratitude helps you close your day on a positive note and reminds you of the bigger picture. Follow that with one thing you learned today and one area where you want to grow tomorrow.

Step 3: Prepare for Tomorrow

Don't just go to bed thinking about tomorrow's to-do list. **Set yourself up for success**. Write down your goals or intentions for the next day. What's your priority? What action will move you closer to your mission?

Step 4: Wind Down Without Technology

Turn off your screen. At least 30 minutes before bed, get off your phone. The blue light from screens messes with your sleep. Do something calming. Read, meditate, or just sit in silence.

Actionable Exercise for Your Evening Ritual:

1. Reflect on your day—what went well, what didn't.
2. Journal for 5-10 minutes (gratitude, insights, growth areas).
3. Prepare for tomorrow (write down your top 3 priorities).
4. Turn off all tech 30 minutes before bed.
5. Wind down—read, meditate, or sit in silence.

4. Consistency: The Secret Sauce

You want to know the key to success? It's **doing the work every single day**. It's in the little actions, the small rituals, the consistency. This isn't about getting it perfect. This is about **doing it consistently**.

The guru's daily ritual isn't a set of perfect practices. It's the dedication to *showing up every day*, no matter what. When you do this, you build momentum. You become the person who **shows up for themselves**. And that's when the transformation happens.

5. Final Thoughts on Rituals and Practice

The guru mindset isn't an accident. It's a result of constant effort and discipline. **Build a practice** that reinforces your goals, your values, and your purpose. The small rituals you create will guide you, anchor you, and provide the structure necessary to achieve the greatness you're after.

Remember, consistency is the key. Start small, build momentum, and **stay committed** to your daily practice. This is how you create the foundation for your guru mindset. It's not an overnight change, but it's a journey that starts with one small ritual at a time.

Get to work.

Appendix 8

The Guru's Role in the Community – Leading with Purpose and Influence

Listen up—this isn't all about you. **If you truly want to embody the guru mindset**, then understand this: **A guru does not exist in a vacuum**. A modern guru doesn't sit on a pedestal waiting for disciples to come to them. A real guru is in the trenches, leading, serving, and influencing the collective consciousness. The guru is the one who doesn't just **master themselves**—they **master their ability to serve others**.

Being a guru means stepping into leadership. **It's about taking responsibility for the well-being of others**, for the health of the community, and for the evolution of the collective. You're not just a lone wolf doing your own thing and feeling good about your personal growth. **A guru understands that their growth is interwoven with the growth of the community.** When the community thrives, you thrive. When you serve, you're elevated. It's not just about you, it's about the bigger picture.

Let's break down how this all works—how you, as a modern guru, can serve your community and make a real impact, all while staying rooted in that calm, clear presence that defines your practice.

1. The Guru as a Leader

The first step in understanding the guru's role in the community is grasping that **true leadership comes from a place of humility, service, and calm presence**. A guru does not lead from ego. A guru does not demand respect. A guru earns it by **walking the talk**—by showing up every day with integrity, discipline, and a commitment to the collective good. They **lead by example**, not through force or authority.

Think about it: If you want to lead, you **must be a servant first**. The guru isn't a dictator; they're a mentor, a guide, and a steward of collective energy. **Your leadership is rooted in serving the greater good**, whether you're working with individuals one-on-one, or leading larger groups toward a common purpose.

Actionable Insight:

If you want to be a leader in your community, stop focusing on *what you're getting out of it*. Focus on *how you're helping others get what they need*. Lead by example. Give your energy, your wisdom, and your time without expecting anything in return. When you give, you will receive.

2. Serving Your Community: A Call to Action

If you are going to live this guru mindset, you need to **serve the people around you**. This isn't an abstract concept—it's real, it's hands-on, and it's necessary for your growth and theirs. **The community is the mirror of the individual**. If you want to see the transformation in yourself, you must help transform others.

Serving your community doesn't always mean grand, heroic gestures. It can be as simple as offering a helping hand to someone in need, providing mentorship to someone who's struggling, or volunteering your time in a way that addresses the issues your community faces. It's about becoming a **source of light in the lives of others**, whether that's through teaching, guiding, or just being present in their struggles.

You want to know how you can make an impact? **Start with what's in front of you**—the people you interact with daily, the circles you move in. Stop waiting for permission to lead. **Step up and serve**. Every time you contribute to the well-being of others, you're contributing to the evolution of collective consciousness. **The guru does not just care for themselves, they care for the collective**.

Here's how you start:

Step 1: Volunteer Your Time

Find a cause, a project, or an initiative that resonates with you. Volunteer your time and skills to support that cause. It could be anything—**helping at a food bank, teaching a class, mentoring youth, or providing professional skills to organizations** that can't afford them.

You might think you don't have the time or energy, but the truth is: **When you give, you multiply your impact.** You'll find that your energy expands as you commit to serving others. You'll also be **surrounded by people who share your values**, and that's how movements start.

Step 2: Lead by Example in Your Work/Business

The guru doesn't just serve outside of work—they **serve within their professional environment** too. **Your role as a leader isn't limited to just what you do in your personal life**—you influence your work, your colleagues, and your employees by how you show up. Do you communicate with empathy and respect? Do you take ownership of your actions and help others rise? Are you holding yourself accountable?

If you're in a position of leadership, use your platform to **create a culture of service, respect, and growth**. Challenge your team to think beyond their own individual needs and contribute to the greater good of the organization and society. Be the example that others follow.

Step 3: Foster Collaboration, Not Competition

A modern guru understands that success is **not a zero-sum game**. When you help others win, you win. So many leaders are stuck in a mentality of competition, of trying to "beat" others, of elevating themselves above the rest. But the guru sees things differently. **The more you help others rise, the more you elevate yourself.**

Encourage collaboration over competition. In your community, in your workplace, or in your family, become the person who fosters connection, who encourages others to join forces, and who helps build a culture of collective growth. A guru doesn't tear others down—they lift them up.

3. Navigating Modern Social Issues with a Guru Mindset

Now, let's get to the heart of the matter. The world is full of **chaos, distractions, and social unrest**. Social media, political divide, environmental collapse, systemic inequality—these are the issues of our time. And if you're going to be a modern guru, you **cannot ignore these issues**.

A guru doesn't retreat from the world, they engage with it—**but they do so with a calm presence, clarity of mind, and a commitment to their principles**. It's about showing up, **without getting lost in the noise**. You cannot change the world if you're consumed by it. But you can influence it through your actions, your calm, and your unwavering commitment to the truth.

Actionable Insight:

- Educate yourself on social and environmental issues. Be informed, not just on the surface level, but deeply.
- Don't get caught in the drama of social media. Take a stand, but do it with **intention**, not just for likes or to be part of a trend.
- **Use your platform to amplify voices** that are often unheard. If you're in a position to lead, whether as an influencer, teacher, or business leader, use your influence to advocate for positive change.

You don't have to lead a revolution to make an impact. Sometimes, it's about **small, consistent actions** that influence change over time.

4. Building Community – The Power of Collective Consciousness

At the end of the day, what makes a guru truly powerful isn't their individual mastery—it's their ability to **create and influence a collective movement**. **The power of the guru lies in their ability to build a community of like-minded individuals who are committed to growth, service, and transformation.**

A community isn't just a group of people. It's a **living, breathing organism** that's only as strong as its members. As a modern guru, your role is to **create, nurture, and lead this community**, helping it evolve into something greater than the sum of its parts.

Actionable Exercise:

- Identify ways you can start creating or enhancing community in your environment. This could mean building a mentoring program, creating a space for discussion on social issues, or simply fostering deeper connections with the people around you.
- Commit to *serving your community* consistently. Volunteer. Mentor. Share your wisdom. Initiate projects. Be the catalyst for positive change.

Conclusion – Your Role in the Collective Evolution

Remember this—**the guru is only as powerful as the community they serve**. Your growth is intrinsically linked to the growth of others. You cannot thrive in isolation. If you truly want to embody the guru mindset, **you must serve the collective**. You must step into leadership roles, serve your community, and create positive change in the world around you. Lead with purpose, communicate with compassion, and stay grounded in your core values.

Now, get out there and make an impact. Your community is waiting.

About Alex Telman

ALEX TELMAN IS A GLOBALLY recognized spiritual healer, author, and one of the country's most read poets. With over 45 years of experience, he has dedicated his life to helping individuals break free from negative energies, trauma, and spiritual blockages. His transformative work has empowered a diverse range of clients, including celebrities, business leaders, educators, and everyday individuals, guiding them toward emotional well-being, personal growth, and spiritual fulfillment.

From an early age, Alex demonstrated extraordinary abilities to perceive and remove harmful energies and entities, a gift that first emerged when he was just three years old. This rare talent led him to study with psychic masters across the globe—Afghanistan, France, Sweden, Israel, England, and Australia—each recognizing his unique gifts and helping him refine his craft.

In addition to his healing practice, Alex has practiced as a barrister, teacher, university lecturer, and small business owner, offering a well-rounded perspective on healing that combines spirituality with practical action. He is also an accomplished author, whose writings inspire and uplift readers by exploring the depths of human emotion and the power of self-healing.

Through his sessions, Alex has helped countless individuals overcome emotional turmoil and reclaim their lives. His work transcends cultural and geographical boundaries, offering profound healing to those in need. His mission is simple yet powerful: to guide people back to their authentic selves, helping them live with purpose, peace, and fulfillment.

With a career built on compassion, wisdom, and deep spiritual insight, Alex remains a beacon of hope for anyone seeking to overcome their struggles and wanting to step into a life of clarity and joy.

Other Titles by Alex Telman

Non Fiction

Mindshift: Change Your Life in 4 Days

Mastering Hypnosis: Complete Step-by-Step Manual, Case Studies, and Sample Scripts

From Cursed to Cured: 100 True Stories of Healing from Curses

Connecting to the Afterlife: a how-to guide

Your Journey from Death to Rebirth

Empower Your Sundays: Unlocking Inner Strength for a Resilient Life

The Truth Behind the Creation Story: A Journey Through Reincarnation

Practical Mentalism in a Nutshell

Reprogram Your Mind in a Nutshell

Meditation in a Nutshell

Alex Telman in Quotes

Novels

Down and Out in Byron Bay

One Life, Half Lived

God Speaks: A Journey Through Creation in His Own Words

Jesus Speaks: The Man Behind the Miracle in His Own Words

Poetry

Echoes of September 11

Homeless in New York

Burning Echoes of Time

From Dawn to Dusk: the life cycle in sonnets

Eternal Echoes: The Tapestry of Time and the Unseen

Snapshots of People I Have Never Met

Legends and Lessons: 36 Myths Unveiled

A Measure of Time: The Eternal Voyage of Self

Ashes of Verses: Poems Burned But Not Forgotten

Telman: The Complete Haiku 1974-2024

Reflections on Solitude: A Poetic Journey Through The Lonely Mind

Your Friendship is a Museum

Whispers to Bella

Don't miss out!

Visit the website below and you can sign up to receive emails whenever Alex Telman publishes a new book. There's no charge and no obligation.

https://books2read.com/r/B-A-YBSCC-WEBLF

BOOKS2READ

Connecting independent readers to independent writers.